DESCENDANTS OF SLAVERY:
ON THE EVENT HORIZON

STEVEN NUR AHMED

authorHOUSE®

AuthorHouse™
1663 Liberty Drive
Bloomington, IN 47403
www.authorhouse.com
Phone: 833-262-8899

Published by AuthorHouse   11/30/2021

ISBN: 978-1-6655-3938-8 (sc)
ISBN: 978-1-6655-3943-2 (e)

Library of Congress Control Number: 2021919653

Print information available on the last page.

This book is printed on acid-free paper.

For All The Slaves Who Died Without
Knowing Their Name

Foreword

After reading Descendants of Slavery: On the Event Horizon, written by Dr. Steven Nur Ahmed, I now understand his natural lean toward activism through story telling. As a seasoned social scientist, theologian, and teacher, Dr. Ahmed uses his lived experiences as a young Black male growing up in the Bay Area of Northern California to illustrate generational connectedness between the past and the present. He addresses trauma and the residual impact of slavery which will no doubt continue to pour over into our future if not interrupted.

As a local civil rights leader, I believe in the power of self-awareness because it is a window into visualizing our greatness and resiliency. However, if you can't see it, it doesn't exist. Dr. Ahmed does a masterful job of turning the lights on by helping us to see clearer the elements of institutionalized racism and its long-term effects intended to keep us in the dark.

His well-written book integrates theory, data, and lived experiences to connect the dots in an easy-to-read format. I particularly appreciate his trusted intellectual leadership during an era of disinformation and alternative facts created to rewrite history and to engineered false truths. People are literally dying due to lack of awareness. I applaud Dr. Ahmed for his continued commitment to social activism and for sharing his research for the greater good.

I challenge you to not only read 'Descendants of Slavery: On the Event Horizon', but to join in the civil rights movement by sharing what you've learned to enlighten others. This book as well as other works by Dr. Steven Nur Ahmed will arm you with credible information and intellectual armor that will help you stand your ground.

Wendy Byrd
President
Modesto/Stanislaus NAACP

Contents

List of Graphs-Photos

Prologue

Dr. Martin Luther King said in a speech 'Fierce Urgency of Now' that "There is such a thing as being too late." I agree with him. I do think time is running out or may have run out for African Americans to mitigate the many environmental and social structural burdens which have shored up against us. I chose the title for this book with that in mind.

I taught Social Science to college students for many years in California. And as a Social Worker I have also been able to directly examine cycles of life and death among African Americans within inner cities. What I have seen over 50 years is what I call the urban entropic effect. It is the ratio of socially enabled descendants of slavery to socially disabled African Americans. It is clear to me now that ratio is biased against both individual and collective socially disabled people on all meaningful levels of social action. For example, in 2002 it was reported that "Nearly a third more African-American men are incarcerated than in higher education[1] That ratio portends economic disaster for descendants of slaves.

There have been alterations in the African American demographic characteristics since the 1990s. We are less culturally monolithic than ever before. The effects of that are observable everywhere. We are less educated relative

[1] Justice Policy Institute, Cellblocks or Classrooms: The Funding of Higher Education and Corrections and its Impact on African American Men, https://justicepolicy.org/research /

to the skills needed to survive today. We are less family oriented today than 50 years ago unless one adapts the postmodern definition of what a family is. We are still at the bottom of all social hierarchies which measure quality of life unless those hierarchies are measures of bad health, proportion of incarcerated men and women, and school dropouts.

I have had a broad range of personal and professional experiences some of which I share in this book. Those experiences have helped me to excavate collective patterns too often neglected or not spoken of in the mainstream media nor taught in high schools, colleges and universities. Now, the well-known phrase 'last hired and the first fired' has a broader meaning for us. It can include now 'at bottom on the social hierarchy, first to suffer extinction'. We, African Americans, are rolling on the event horizon. I hope it is not too late.

1

American Aryanism

I have carefully sifted through the varied threads of thought in the founding documents of English colonies as well as state and federal governments. In so doing, I have observed one very unusual thread which unites all the documents. It was and is 16th century imperial racism. That single thread was sewn into the very fabric of every colonial, federal and state constitution for over 243 years. Indeed, it started the countdown to violent rebellions, civil war, the cry for civil rights, assassinations, and a continually seething social discontent in descendants of slavery and indeed in all the modern nations of Europe, Africa, Australia, and the Americas.

If John Locke was right when he wrote that we are born 'tabula rasa' then within four slave generations after 1619 our collective memories and traditions were nearly wiped out. For example, it was impossible for me to know in my childhood that my life chances were a function of imperial competition between Portugal, Holland, Germany, England, France, Spain, and the United States. When the U.S. was founded, no one in my family lineage could read or write because it was against states' laws for slaves to read and write. Slaves literally didn't even know their names. That was 243 years ago. It has taken over 200 years for some African Americans to learn to read and write, but we will never know our names. That is a common narrative of African Americans throughout the United States today. So, it seems that at least descendants of slavery were born as Locke theorized 'tabula rasa'.

It was impossible for any of our ancestors to have understood that they were the victims of a world view applied as capitalism and a resurrected form of white supremacy or ancient Aryanism.[2] Slave plantations were not only concentration labor camps, but slaves were also captives in what sociologist Irving Goffman defined as a 'total institution' of indoctrination.[3] The food slaves were forced to eat was garbage and what they were told about themselves both individually and as a group in relation to the world was garbage. It was a classical psychological operation. Isolate Africans, segregate Africans, and eliminate all knowledge of self then replace knowledge of self with garbage.

In my youth, I never heard the name Aryan (e-re-uhn) openly mentioned in schools I attended. None of my teachers K thru 12 or University professors mentioned Aryanism in their lectures unless it was narrowly applied to Adolf Hitler's race propaganda against Jews or his 'National Socialist German Workers Party' ideology. The word was never defined. We were not taught that it was a

---

[2] The word Aryan is an Indo-European word in the language of Sanskrit. It means 'Superior', 'Civilized', or 'Socialized'.

[3] Goffman, Irving, Asylums: Essays on the Social Situation of Mental Patients on Other Inmates, Anchor Books, 1961

global religious movement cloaked as ideology or in the form of modern Christianity.[4]

The Aryan religion has been implied in every repressive act or act of omission against African Americans, Indigenous peoples, and Latinos in the United States. Christianity, for example, is a benign form of Aryanism because it implies two ideas.[5] The benign methodology is to inform us through images and mythologies which excite and entertain us. The European version of Christianity implies that if you are not a Christian then you are inferior and damned. And, that if you are non-white, you cannot ever be equal to white people. Those two hidden assumptions are deeply embedded within the non-white individual and their collective subconscious world view. That makes everyone to some degree a white supremacist.

All people in the United States are socialized to be white supremacists. Today, their indoctrination is usually benign. It is done to them in ways that are non-threatening and entertaining. Ways that are made pleasant or pleasurable experiences. The forums are mass interpersonal interactions like public and private schools. But also, through impersonal media interactions twenty-four hours seven days a week in both imagery and print.

Most people don't even know when indoctrination is happening to them. It is astounding that a whole population is literally put into automatic sleep-walk through life. They

---

[4] I distinguish between modern Christianity and what the Prophet Jesus taught.

[5] Poliakov, Leon, The Aryan Myth; Barnes & Noble's Books, New York, 1971

substitute their predetermined 'world view' for reality. Pretending that their world view is reality they respond to it in relation to others and the environment. For instance, just recently a mass grave of 751 indigenous children in Canada was unearthed adjacent to a Catholic Boarding school which operated from 1896 to 1998.[6] In the boarding school the children were forced to accept Christianity and to assimilate Canadian culture by not using their language and dressing in their traditional clothing. The children were subject to operant conditioning because they were beaten and abused to force them to conform. What happened to those children was not an example of what the Teacher from Nazareth taught and practiced. It was the methodology of Aryanism which had coopted Christianity in Europe and had spread throughout the Americas.

White supremacy is a synonym for what was and is called in the Hindu language of Sanskrit the 'Aryan' caste. The noun 'Aryan' was in vogue during the 'Age of Enlightenment'. In the 16th century, European intellectuals who were anti-Christian, anti-African and anti-Semitic advocated it as their ancient pagan religion as it had been advocated in India for over two thousand years. In 1775, Johann Blumenbach proclaimed 'Caucasians' to be the 'beautiful' race as does Hinduism.[7] Slowly but surely Aryanism infiltrated the University curricula of both religious and secular colleges in Europe and the United

---

[6] Saskatchewan, Canada, June 2021, New York Times

[7] Blumenbach, Johann, On the Natural Origin of Human Variety; 1775; see: Jefferson, Thomas; Notes On the State of Virginia-Query 14, 1782

States. It eventually came to be the popular world view of every secular institution and Christian denomination in Europe and the Americas.[8] Believers in Aryanism and in whatever form it takes claim blatantly or indirectly racial superiority.[9]

They claim their 'whiteness' to be proof of their individual and collective superiority. They claim that God is a white man not verbally but with pictures. They use still and motion pictures to suggest that idea to all children who pass through their institutions. They believe that their children must be marked for life by skin color. Kenneth and Mamie Clark proved the life-time damage 'marking' does to young children with their baby doll selection experiment.[10] We can see the life-time effects in black or white adults who act out the conditioned world view they experienced as young children through some of their most important life choices.

The fundamental premise of Aryanism is in the original Hindu catechism 'The Law Code of Manu'. They claim that their race was made by a god named Purusha. The English noun 'Mankind" is derived from the Sanskrit

---

[8] Even the celebrated Emanual Kant was a believer in the Hindu Code of Manu: see "Immanuel Kant in Bernasconi, Robert, "Kant as An Unfamiliar Source of Racism," *Philosophers on Race: Critical Essays*, Julie K. Ward & Tommy L. Lott, editors, Malden, Massachusetts, Blackwell, 2002, 145–166; 148.

[9] "The Age of Enlightenment was an intellectual and philosophical movement that dominated the world of ideas in Europe during the 17th and 18th centuries." Wikipedia

[10] Clark, Kenneth and Clark, Mamie P., Racial Identification and Preference in Negro Children, Socialization of the Child, pp.169-178

noun Manu. So, whenever you say 'Man' you are saying 'Manu'.[11] Linguistic psychological manipulation and control over us is deep. How can one escape the language he or she uses?

Critical race theory is a sub-branch of the sociology of knowledge. It is the exploration and deconstruction of race ideology. For that reason, it is dangerous to white supremacists' power structures. In the past, the indoctrination of children into white supremacy was direct and up front. Throughout its history Americans have been arrogantly blatant and hostile white supremacists. America was legally or de facto segregated. Segregation served their ongoing indoctrination process well. Even in Washington D.C., there were white and black drinking fountains, hotels, taxi cabs, and schools. Segregation reinforced the elite racial caste hierarchical world view established by the U.S. Constitution. That in turn created white privilege or preferential treatment and concentrated wealth and political power in the white population in perpetuity.

At least half of the white people in the United States consciously do not want what they call 'Critical Race Theory' taught in k-12 schools nor at Universities and Colleges. Many of them are actively involved in censorship efforts to curtail free speech on campuses across the nation. Seventy-four million people voted for

---

[11] "Etymology of man. It is derived from a Proto-Indo-European root 'man-(see Sanskrit/Avestan manu-, Slavic Moz "man, male"). In Hindu mythology, Manu is the name of the traditional progenitor of humankind who survives a deluge and gives mankind laws." Man (word)-Wikipedia

Donald Trump in the 2020 presidential election. When he lost the presidential race there was a mass rebellion in Washington D.C. on January 6, 2020. It is a particularly delicate procedure to benignly socialize people because there is a need to maximize control over the environment as much as possible without it being known that it is being done. People are not supposed to look at the fourth wall as they are being benignly trained to dramatize their 'whiteness'.

It is institutionally important that the indoctrination process is done as thoroughly and competently as possible because they depend upon it to engage their children emotionally and psychologically in their formative years. Thus, any facts which contradict white supremacist's mythology in the habitat of their children will to some degree weaken the circuit of the whiteness indoctrination process. That in turn has far reaching ripple effects on the fabric of society spanning decades and centuries.

New facts which contradict the myth of white supremacy will change the world view of children once they are exposed to such facts. It will crack and shatter the Aryan paradigm because the assumptions of Aryanism are false. Trillions of tons in gold and silver as well as trillions in currency will be transferred from the power elite to the oppressed. That will level the playing field so that all people can have a better life chance at birth. Thus, simple fairness will end white privilege and the racial hierarchy that should have been buried centuries years ago.

Most Americans are spurred to action by a comparatively small percentage of white intellectuals who are 'all weather bigots' or white supremacists.[12] They operate at every level in society but most importantly they operate at the very centers of power which for centuries has allowed them to be the gate keepers who determine what is taught and who will teach their children and control media. It is that group of white supremacists who denied tenure to Hannah Jones.

Hannah Jones is one of the authors of the 1619 Project published by the New York Times. She was recently denied tenure in the Journalism department at the University of North Carolina at Chapel Hill. Her tenure denial is an example of academic censorship at the highest centers of intellectual training.

The action by the Board of Trustees is not a new tenure posture of UNC Chapel Hill or at other Universities or colleges because the denial and denigration of black scholars in academia is yet another characteristic of the African American experience in the United States. It is used to intimidate non-white scholars to control their lecture content, research interests or social activism off campus.

Have you ever wondered why grass root social movements led by college professors rarely if ever start on University and College campuses? It is because the hiring and tenure committees and boards of trustee on college campuses are all arch conservatives and hire like-minded and like looking individuals. It is no wonder that

---

[12] Merton, R. K. (1949). Discrimination and the American creed. In R. M. MacIver (Ed.), *Discrimination and national welfare* (pp. 99–126). New York, NY: Harper and Row

institutions of higher education function to churn out intellectuals bound in mental strait jackets.

Liberal Arts, Political Science, and Social Science faculty spend most of their time competing for grants, publishing arcane articles or books, and regurgitating a white supremacist world view of history and the contemporary world to their students, even if only impliedly. Black Ph.D. faculty constitutes maybe 2.5 percent of the Ph.Ds. awarded and spend most of their careers teaching white and Asian children in large Universities.[13] Black people do not benefit from black Ph.D. recipients. They teach or serve in various administrative roles usually in education like the Indian functionaries under the British Raj, then most retire on a pension, and disappear.

But the denial of Hannah Jones was influenced by an executive order called the "The 1776 Commission" signed by Donald Trump. He described 'Critical Race Theory' as being ideologically 'toxic propaganda' to the bond which holds Americans together.[14] It was repealed by President Joseph Biden.[15] Now, states' legislatures have taken censorship postures to suppress critical historical accounts of United State history like 'Black History'. Sixteen states including Texas, Idaho, Oklahoma, Iowa, Tennessee have either passed laws or are in the process of passing laws to prohibit teaching fact-based history.

---

[13] The HBCU colleges do matriculate more Descendants of Slavery. But the presence of African American Males has been decreasing for years.

[14] Map: Where Critical Race Theory Is Under Attack

[15] Map: Where Critical Race Theory Is Under Attack

So, what is it all about? Is it about Critical Race Theory? I would say yes but only in part. I think that the states cited above are desperately trying to continue damaging young white children by socializing them to be white supremacists. Their goal is to reinstitute a public brand of 'American Aryanism' as it was intended to be as written about in 1788 through states' legislation and, if necessary, by civil war.

2

America is Based on a Slave Model

A German Social scientist named Max Weber formulated a theory he called 'Life Chances'.[16] He stated life chances are "the opportunities that each individual has to improve their quality of life." And that there are three unavoidable life situations each of us are born into. Those life situations determine our individual life chances and in so doing our quality of life. The three situations are 1) family income, 2) parents' education level, and 3) their health. At birth, descendants of slaves fall far below the median level in each life situation. Thus, the probability that the vast majority of African Americans will achieve the middle class is low to zero.

The United States was not designed so that descendants of slavery could ever achieve income and wealth parity with middle class white Americans. And the existing wealth and income gap between whites and descendants of slavery proves that to be true. Statistically, the income gap between African Americans and whites can only widen. Equity is growth whereas no equity is zero growth.

---

[16] Max Weber, Economy and Society: An Outline of Interpretive Sociology; University of California Press, 1922

There are hundreds of social statistical measures which could be used to support my claim. But suffice it to say that the chances that a black person will make it to the middle class is slight. A middle-class income for people ages 25-54 ranges between a minimum of $37,000.00 and a maximum of $147,000.00 per year.[17] Only 12% of the people in the middle-class range of incomes are African American compared to 49% for whites. That is 4 times more white people in the middle class than African Americans. But what should also be kept in mind is that not all African Americans in the middle class are descendants of slavery.

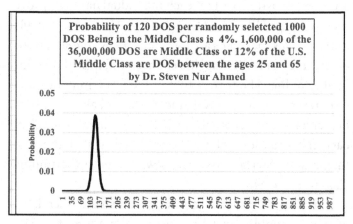

Figure 1

A growing percentage of middle-class African Americans are immigrants or their descendants. Their median income, wealth, and education levels are higher than that of descendants of slaves. A few basic

---

[17] Brookings Institute: Year: 2019

political and economic facts will help to flush out my claim. Inflation, lack of accumulated equity assets, and destruction of culture are reasons that have made it impossible for descendants of slavery to close the wealth gap with white Americans.[18] A reparations mechanism to freed slaves like that of 'General order #15' could have narrowed the present wealth gap, but when it was repealed by Andrew Johnson made it impossible for freed slaves to get economic traction and thus parity with whites.[19]

A person could buy a candy bar for .5 cents in 1960. I know because I bought many of those .5 cent candy bars. Today, in 2013, that same candy bar cost $1.00. Over a timespan of 53 years, a candy bar cost 20 times more than it did in 1960. The same can be said for home costs. In 1970, a four-bedroom home in the Oakland foothills could be purchased for about $20,000.00 with a down payment of 10% or $2,000.00. Interest rates were fixed at 3% for 30 years.

Most African Americans could not buy a home in Oakland, San Francisco, or Los Angeles in the 20th century because of low income, redlining, restrictive covenants, or home loan discrimination by banks.[20] That compelled them to rent and thereby grow property equity for white rental property owners and of course to accumulate debt. It's nearly impossible for African Americans to get freed from the share cropping business model.

The same home I mentioned would cost today over

---

[18] See: Murder on the Yard

[19] Abraham Lincoln issued to General Sherman Special Field Orders #15 in 1865 ordering him to distribute

[20] Richard Rothstein, The Color of Law, Liveright Publishing Corporation,, New York, 2017

$500,000.00 dollars. So, people who bought homes in the 1940s, 1950s, 1960s and 70s earned substantially more equity per year as compared to the inflation rate. Many white children benefited financially by inheriting the equity in their parents' homes. Inheriting equity is a hedge against the declining value of the dollar due to inflation. Thus, the children of homeowners are more likely to become homeowners or pay their college tuition to avoid student loans in today's market. Equity or inheritance maintains the uniformity of the socio-economic hierarchy.

Those who got into asset building first like white homesteaders in the 19th century and bequeathed their assets to their descendants via inheritance and white privilege tend to stay on top. Conversely, those who got into asset building last or never did get life-long credit debt or homelessness.[21] One must have assets to move up to higher asset levels.

We could do the same calculation for bread, milk, eggs, houses, rentals, and gasoline. For example, a loaf of bread cost about .20 cents in 1960. Now, that same loaf of bread will cost us about $4.00 dollars. That's about 20 times more than it cost in 1960. I paid about $115.00 a month for a two-bedroom apartment in 1970. That same apartment today will cost 10 times more or slightly less depending upon its location. I think you get my point. Inflation eats away at the purchasing power of the dollar. If you don't get an annual cost of living raise of at least 3% or cut your cost by an annual rate of 3% then you fall behind. The dollar will look the same but it ain't the same.

The cost of living tends to always increase. For

---

[21] "The future tends to replicate the past."

example, the energy necessary for a person to expend to do work increases as they age because people naturally weaken as they age. That is the cost of living. As the dollar ages, it cost more of them to do the same work. But there is an added cost for living incurred by descendants of slavery. Historically we have had a collective poverty rate consistently greater than 2 times that of whites because we are of African descent.

The poverty ownership ratio between descendants of slaves and whites stretching back to 1964 has made life tenuous for over 21% of descendants of slaves in the United States considering health problems and now the Covid-19 pandemic.[22] Every day, descendants of slavery fall further and further behind in the quality of their lives and length of their lifespans because of inflation in relation to their stagnant incomes. Minimum wage increases are not enough.

I think that the only solution is reparations from the Federal government. Only it can level the economic playing field. Figure-2 demonstrates that the white to black poverty ratio of 2 blacks for every 1 white remained constant throughout the Obama tenure. Yet, another example of what Derrick Bell argued when he stated that there is progress but no change.

---

[22] Figure-2 describes the poverty variance between blacks and whites to be 2.7 blacks for every 1 white during the Obama administration.

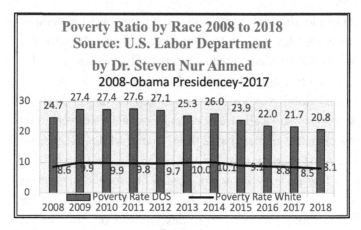

Figure 2

The costs of commodities increase in relation to the annual inflation rate too. The annual inflation rate has averaged 3% per year for over 100 years. All businesses try to grow their profit margins in relation to the increased cost of living. That means that if your annual income has not increased at a rate at least equal to that of the annual inflation rate then each dollar you earn or save will decrease in value approximately 3% per year. Consequently, you will not be able to keep up with the cost of living; instead, you will be getting poorer though the dollar will always look the same. The minimum wage was designed to be a pacification policy to protect the government from rebellion, not for its citizens. It still is. Increases in minimum wages will always be passed on to consumers. The net result is increases in minimum wages do not make a difference in the purchasing power of poor people.

The first Federal minimum wage was set at .25 cents per hour in 1938 during the great depression. It was part of the 'New Deal' signed into law by Franklin D. Roosevelt.

Today, the minimum wage set by the Federal Government is $13.00 dollars per hour though states can set it higher. For instance, in California, it is $14.00 dollars per hour for employers with 26 or more employees and $13.00 dollars per hour for employers with 25 or fewer employees.

The Federal minimum wage has increased 52 x .25 = $13.00/hr. from what it was in 1938. Some states are moving toward 15.00 dollars an hour minimum wage. But by the time the new hourly minimum wage is in place in most places, annual inflation rates will have devalued the dollar even more resulting in far less cost-of-living gain than anticipated. If commodity and retail prices as well as interest rates had increased at a slower rate and if African Americans had received reparations for slavery, then more African Americans would be in the middle class instead of a paltry 12% compared to 49% of white people. It is a virtual certainty that most descendants of slaves will live out their lives at the bottom of the social hierarchy no matter how hard they try not to.

The structure of the economy is circular like a ring of dominos. At one end the 'invisible hand' pushes down the first domino. The first domino transfers its weight plus momentum when it pushes down the second and so on and so on. Costs are likewise transferred with incremental increases in costs from raw resource abstractors to manufacturers to distributors to wholesalers to retailers and finally to consumers. But there is little to no balancing reverse push today because the balancing circuit has been broken by the exodus of capital out of the United States.

Unionized workers once played the role of a balancing reverse power that pushed costs back to companies though most African Americans were not allowed into unions initially. But now only 10.8% of all workers are in unions compared to 25% of workers in 1955. Here, again, black workers were last in line. Descendants of slavery did not fully benefit from unionization in the early and mid- 20th century because Unions were controlled by white supremacist who discriminated against them and validated the legal segregation of black people. So, when unions started at the end of the 18th and beginning of the 20th centuries finally reaching their peak in 1954 at 35%, black workers were only a small fraction of that number. We missed the union buffet. We were last and least.

Descendants of slavery are always hit hardest like lower caste Dalits in India.[23] The only way to beat the odds and come out ahead is to either get an annual cost of living raise above 3% or get a second job. The function of the system cannot be fair or just toward black people and very little toward other ethnic groups because injustice or the perpetuation of imbalance in the marketplaces is necessary to maintain an oligarchic caste hierarchy.

The system operates according to its design. Racial order is important in our system, too. There are limited opportunities from highest to lowest; either you find one of the limited places in the system or you are 'outcaste'. For example, look at the graph below. Descendants of slavery are situated in lower income unskilled jobs in the labor force. It reflects one of several ways education, income, and wealth are distributed unequally by race.

---

[23] Dalit means 'broken'. They are the outcaste of India created by Hinduism. They are the indigenous black people of India.

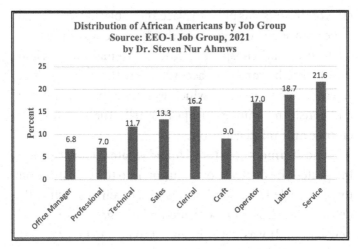

Figure 3

Colonial American was clear about their design for a racial order from high racial caste to low racial caste. One hundred and thirty-eight years before the Declaration of Independence (1776) the Maryland Colony Council wrote this:

> "Neither the existing black population nor any other Blacks shall be permitted to enjoy the fruits of White society.[24]

The doctrine was enforced by state police power and would later exclude Irish immigrants by degree as indentured servants.[25] We are therefore forced to admit that a legally defined permanent underclass and lower-

---

[24] Doctrine of Exclusion, Maryland Colony Council, 1638
[25] White Trash: The 400-Year Untold History of Class in America, by Nancy Isenberg, Penguin Books, 2016

class of laborers was put into place and subjected to colonial police power. The purpose of the doctrine was threefold: 1.) To profit off cheap labor cost, 2.) To maintain a rigid racial caste hierarchy in accordance with the religion of Aryan white supremacy which was being propagandized and spreading among European intellectuals and 3.) To enforce anti-miscegenation.

The framers of the United States Constitution integrated the doctrine of exclusion into the Constitution under Article 1, Section 2, Clause 3. Therein it specifically defines the class and caste hierarchy/oligarchy of 'their' new nation. It was never intended to be a democracy. At the bottom of the hierarchy are the same ethnic groups mentioned in the Doctrine of Exclusion. Those bound for service meaning indentured European immigrants, Indigenous Tribes, and Africans who were relegated to be a permanent caste (3/5ths all others).[26] The United States was predicated on inequality otherwise it could not function as a nation then nor now.

The obvious intent of the founders was to legalize slavery by race. They also intended to construct a lower class of dependent laborers which would be comprised of poor ethnic European immigrants. They reasoned as did the ancient Romans that in an agriculturally based economy the most efficient and fastest way for a dominate caste of oligarchs to generate profit and accumulate wealth was by cheap and free labor. Most of them had read Aristotle's book 'Politics' wherein he states that democracy gives power to poor people and thus is not a good form of

---

[26] The appropriate designation for slaves is African or their tribal affiliation because they were not citizens.

government and that some people or groups are naturally disposed to be slaves and while others are disposed to be slave-masters.[27]

But slavery ended in the United States, and a new set of socio/economic issues arose. One issue is the growing permanent underclass which cuts across all ethnic, age, and gender boundaries. We can see it in the face of the growing homeless population in major cities and rural areas across the nation. That population is comprised mainly of 'baby boomers' who are retired and cannot live off social security.

The technological revolution and cheap overseas laborers, especially in robotics, has made millions of American laborers obsolete. Generation X, Millennials, and Gen Z will follow in line the homeless baby boomers into what can only be described as the awakening at the edge of the great American mirage.[28] Despite that many conservative thinkers continue to believe that labor exploitation is necessary and should remain the fundamental operating premise in the marketplaces of America. There is no bottom to their avarice.

That leads to what I think is an obvious conclusion. The modern underclass is no longer needed except in marginal kinds of employment like agriculture and food service industries like eateries, etc. Now, as their expectations are

---

[27] "In a democracy the poor will have more power than the rich, because there are more of them, and the will of the majority is supreme." Aristotle, Politics

[28] Rifkin, Jeremy, The End of Work: The Decline of the Global Labor Force and the Dawn of the Post-Market Era; Putman's, New York, 1995

not met their frustrations increase. Millions of Americans will be identified as national security threats to the power elite.[29] America is on track to become a dysfunctional totalitarian state. Where does all that leave descendants of slavery? Tragically, it leaves all of us in the most tenuous circumstance we've ever been in since the civil war. Generally, our life chances are approaching zero. If you think that is a too sweeping a generalization, I beg to differ with you. Just factor in catastrophic climate change happening right now all around you and I think you'll get a glimpse of the big picture. My conclusion is that the only immediate solution for descendants of slavery is cash reparations.

---

[29] Dollard, John, Miller, Doob, Mowrer, Orval, Sears, Robert, Frustration and Aggression; Yale University Press, 1939

3

The Absence of Intent

There is a dangerous myth circulating among African Americans. It is perpetuated on You-tube channels by black historical revisionists with questionable political associations. It is the myth that African slaves built the United States. Whether the myth originated as intentional deceit or ignorance on their part I do not know. But what I do know is that many undereducated young African Americans like to hear that myth because it makes them feel good.

I think the myth, the lie, should be debunked because if one claims that slaves were the 'builders' then that implies their intent to do labor as slaves for no wages. Furthermore, it implies the slaves had an economic stake in the United States. It suggests that they had something to gain and that they were responsible actors along-side the slave-master. Of course, all of that is absurd and it weakens the argument for reparations for descendants of slaves.

The statement by some that "slaves built it [pre-civil war U.S.] with their labor" equates the subject of the statement 'slaves' with the predicate 'it' ['pre-civil war U.S.] with their [possessive case] labor [energy]'. The implication is that slaves 'possessed themselves' and were the intentional co-builders of the pre-civil war U.S. freely giving of their energies. There are obvious logical inconsistencies with that historical narrative.

First, either the statement is true or false. It cannot be both true and false. My argument is that the statement is false for the following reasons. The word 'chattel' means movable legal personal property. Slaves were legally defined as chattel. As such, slaves were governed under property law not the Bill of Rights which protected citizens as stated in the U.S. Constitution. Slave masters could move slaves at their discretion like inmates in a prison. Thus, neither in colonial America nor up until after the Thirteenth Amendment to the Constitution was ratified did slaves possess themselves as Free Persons or agents unless they were convicted of a felony.

When a person makes such a rhetorical claim his or her intent is to emotionally manipulate their audience. To do so, the speaker intentionally commits the fallacy of amphiboly or using a grammatically ambiguous statement to arouse sentimental support for their idea. The fact is that enslaved Africans were the legal property of white supremacists. Under the law, even if a slave escaped from a slave holding state to a non-slave holding state, slaves were not recognized as free persons or agents as was decided by the Supreme Court when it upheld the slave status of Dred Scott in Missouri in the case Dred Scott v. Sanford, 1854.

Secondly, a mule and a slave or any other domesticated animal on a slave plantation in the antebellum south had the same legal status. Now when a mule is hitched up to pull a plow, the mule is more related to the plow than to the plowman because both the mule pulling the plow and the plow are no more than tools. But neither the plow nor the mule is legally identical nor even like the plowman because the plowman is not a tool used by another person nor is he/she the property of another person or group of people. From that, it follows necessarily that neither the mule nor the slave is the farmer. But it also follows necessarily that both the mule and the slave are exploited for free use of their energy or work or labor aside from minimal cost for upkeep.

Even more so, it is the farmer who sows his seed onto the furrowed land. The mule does not sow its seed onto the land. We cannot say that the crops (wealth or added value to the farm) which grow are the product of the mule. Thus, within the context of capitalism we cannot say that slaves working in any capacity for a slave master are builders of a plantation or its fixtures nor the owners of the added value or wealth which grows because of the exploitation of their labor.

The ideology of capitalism defines the owner/chattel relation to be the absolute exploitation of slave energy by 'its' owner. It is the owner(s) who is/are the farmer(s). Under such conditions, the only viable option for the slave to become a self-possessive free agent is to rebel and overthrow his owner by any means necessary. There is no legal way out of slavery because the law is written by slave masters to serve their purposes for slaves, the only viable solution for slaves is to kill all those in the slave master caste because the slave has no redress rights at law. No doubt that after generations of illiteracy and formation of slave habits it would take an unlikely major leap of self-consciousness to reach the conclusion that slave rebellion is the only option. I can think of only one nonlethal option and that is for slaves to morally disregard slave masters' claims to legal property rights. In other words, slaves would have to take possession (loot) or destroy all the master's property.

Lastly, ownership or the title 'builder' must be tracible back to 'intent'. If one person or a group of persons who form the intent to commit an act and then gather all the resources necessary to actualize their intent by the efficient use of their 'tools' whether such tools are organic ones or inorganic is/are the builders. This problem is only resolvable with an analysis of intent.

No slave who was brought to the Americas formed an 'intent' to leave their homeland to come to the Americas. They were kidnaped and held on slave ships under duress. Africans were brought to the Americas involuntarily. Involuntary behavior is the opposite of intentional behavior. A knee jerk is not a 'kick'. A knee jerk is an unconscious reflex.

For example, if we trace the footsteps of one slave back to the slave loading docks or even back to his or her village, that person before his or her capture will not have formed the intent to come to the colonies or the United States let alone 'to build' anything for white people in the United States. Thus, those who were enslaved could never form 'intent' to do any act of their own inherent free will while living on a slave ship or on a slave plantation because the long chain of involuntary acts stretching back generations determined by their owners' absolute control of their bodies and their consciousness in the Americas preempted their intent.

It was the intent of the slave-master that was the driver of slave labor from sunup till sundown. It was part and parcel of the dehumanization of Africans, i.e., to deprive them of inherent intentional behavior or the freedom to be self-determinate. Slaves did not build the pre-civil United States; slaves did not intend to suffer on plantations. On the contrary, slaves were unwilling victims of intimidation, the terror of violence, unimaginable emotional and physical distress, and never-ending suffering. The damages done to them are indisputable. Under any court of justice, they and their descendants would have a rightful claim to seek remedy and monetary as well as punitive damages from the governments which by law cause pain, suffering, and death to them.

So, we do not need a myth to justify our right to reparations in the form of monetary damages for all descendants of slavery. All that we need to do is to put forth the facts. The hard facts. Facts which describe a racial caste system dating back to the founding of the U.S. and institutionalized in its Constitution. Facts which qualify each and every descendant of slaves a rendering of justice.

Rhetorical speeches can be emotionally persuasive, but their premises are always fallacious. Because of their emotionalism they scramble the brains of listeners by constructing the myth that 'slaves-built America'. Those who are not confused reject rhetorical speeches. They are not needed to pursue justice.

Even those with good intentions have failed to understand that social justice movements must be based upon historical facts and led by competent and cogent thinking leaders otherwise such movements are doomed to fail from the start.

4

Criminal Justice is a Banking System

The criminal justice system is a financial banking system. It banks human flesh from entrance to exit and then back into both jails and prisons. Ninety-seven percent of federal arrestees' and ninety-four percent of state arrestee's plea bargain with district attorneys and thus never have their day in court.[30] Most arrestees are functionally illiterate. The criminal justice system takes advantage of that and functions on a business for profit model. It is the hidden paradigm which drives the whole system. Within both the short and long run, it aims to profit monetarily by cycling human flesh through its infrastructures.

We have all been influenced by the steady stream of propaganda that our criminal justice system is here to protect us from crime. That our streets are overrun with criminals. That police and prisons are the only lines of defense. That police need funding for weapons of warfare

---

[30] Prisons Are Packed Because Prosecutors Are Coercing Plea Deals And, Yes, It's Totally Legal., by Clark Neily, August 8, 2019, The CATO INSTITUTE

on our streets. We are relentlessly bombarded twenty-four hours seven days a week by media and the internet imagery that triggers anxiety in the public with every passing criminal incident in the United States and the world. Television shows and movies reinforce the images by glorifying the work of detectives, police officers, and our criminal courts in the war against crime.

But the glaring truth is that we are less protected and thus more insecure in California than ever before. The reason is because the criminal justice system has become a ubiquitous infringer of our civil rights and a disturber of public peace. The criminal justice system is not working for us it is a self-perpetuating institution protecting its interests. It is a racket not unlike that which General Smedley D. Butler wrote about in his book: War is a Racket.[31] How is it that African Americans constitute about 5.6% of California's population but 29% of California's State prison population? (see figure 4 end of chapter)

The answer is simple and generally well know. The criminal justice system was designed to profile descendants of slavery and lock them up to exploit them. The county jail chain gangs which were born out of black codes started in Mississippi and Georgia and then spread throughout southern states. Like black codes, they were enacted to scramble the lives of freed slaves just as they had done to plantation slaves. And, yes, it was all to maintain human trafficking.[32]

---

[31] Smedley D. Butler, War is a Racket, pub. Feral House, 2003

[32] Dan Moore, Sr. & Michele Mitchell, Black Codes In Georgia, pub. The APEX Museum, 2006

It was all done to exploit human flesh for economic gain. Just like every war America has been in, economic gains flowed into every nook and cranny of the United States economy to grow the power of white supremacy and what would become police officers on the street to wardens supervising prisons to the parole and probation officers managing the tens of thousands of socially disabled people in our cities. We have long passed the tipping point and thus have triggered the urban entropic effect.

According to the California Innocence Project, "…a 2012 report by the California Department of Corrections and rehabilitation, more than 65 percent of those released from California's prison system return within three years. Seventy-three percent of the recidivist committed a new crime or violated parole within the first year."[33] The failure to rehabilitate a reasonable number of incarcerated people has been yet another iteration of the failure of the criminal justice system. It has been a failure at the expense of everyone in the state of California and indeed the nation. But the point is that it is a cash cow. It is a money-making system costing taxpayers billions of dollars per year. To put it bluntly, the justice system is a human trafficking hustle under the color of law. Let me explain how it works.

The California prison population has been maintained at a near constant population for 10 years. Despite a federal court order to decrease its prison population, it has shuffled thousands of its non-violent offenders into county jails where they do their time. So, the per diem rate

---

[33] California Innocence Project,
https://californiainnocenceproject.org

of pay per person remains constant in the system.[34] As of April 2020, 132,070 people were incarcerated according to the CDCR but not necessarily in one of its 33 prisons. That means that at that time the CDCR had yet to conform to the design capacity ordered by the federal court. In 2010 it was at 13.75% of the design capacity of 79, 828 individuals.

The CDCR is over the 106, 024 limit ordered by the court. It cost is staggering. It cost about $81,203 per year to incarcerate a man or women in California State prisons in 2018-19.[35] That amounts to $9,500,751,000.00 (billion dollars) per year paid out of the public treasury. So, hypothetically, if a person had a 9-billion-dollar principal in the bank (prison system) at the start of the year and a statically guaranteed 65% recidivist rate (interest) of reentry that translates into a compound interest rate of $5,850,000,000.00 (five billion dollars) per 2 to 3 years. That would pump the principal up to $14,850,000,000.00 in 2 or 3 years and the interest cycle of 65% (those who return to prison) would remain constant!

Now, to make up for any dip in the 65% recidivist rate there are the first-timers or people who enter prison for the first time. First timers keep the 'interest' rate constant if there are any dips in arrest rates. So, it all depends

---

[34] BROWN, GOVERNOR OF CALIFORNIA, ET AL. v. PLATA ET AL., 2010; In a landmark ruling, a federal three-judge panel ordered the California Department of Corrections and Rehabilitation (CDCR) to cap the prison population of its 33 adult prisons to 13.75% of their 79, 828 design capacity, or 109,763 prisoners, within two years. By Marvin Mentor, September 2009, Prison Legal News.

[35] Legislative Analyst's Office, The California Legislature's Nonpartisan Fiscal and Policy Advisor

upon a robust arrest rate which stands at about 1.2 million persons per year from every city and town in California. Who benefits? I stated that we are in the grip of the urban entropic effect, so I think I should say first none of us benefit. Our inner-city communities are degraded. There is no nice way to say it. The ratio of socially enabled to socially disabled African Americans is biased in favor of socially disabled individuals in neighborhoods and whole communities. Rehabilitation has failed in California and in most states is not a goal of prison systems.

Those who do benefit in a very one-dimensional way are all the people who work in the criminal justice system. They are those who never look beyond their next paycheck, promotion, or retirement pension. They simply don't care about the long-term effects to people or communities and that their employer traffics in human bodies for profit. And, yes, private companies and for-profit prisons benefit too. They make hundreds of millions of taxpayer dollars via contracts with the State of California. The same happens across the nation.

The thesis of this chapter is that contrary to what we have been made to believe, the criminal justice system is a banking business. It traffics in human bodies and banks them in prisons and jails. I'm not saying that there aren't very bad people that must be delt with, but what I am saying is that we have social structural problems which for African Americans and Latinos have been designed or allowed to falter to increase the probability that one out of three of our children will ride the school pipeline to prison slide and become lifelong socially disabled persons.

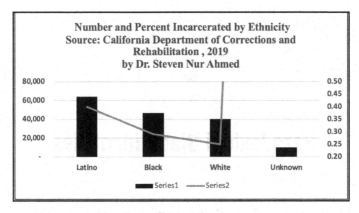

Figure 4

5

Paradoxical Black Identities

Eric Garner died of a chokehold put on him by New York police officer Daniel Pantaleo on July 17, 2014. At the scene of the killing, Pantaleo had suspected Garner was in the commission of the crime…selling untaxed single cigarettes on a street corner. Most of you think Garner died in the New York City Borough of Staten Island. Well, yes and no. I have what I think is a more precise explanation of where Eric Garner's killing occurred.

But first let me prep you just a little for my explanation. For years I've told my students to trace behavior back to the cause of a person's act, i.e., their intention. A sociologist by the name of Max Weber defined 'social action' as an act intended to convey meaning.[36] What he meant by that definition is that if meaning is not conveyed to another person or group then it does not qualify as a social action. Rather it is more likely a meaningless knee jerk reaction to something. Crimes of passion fall into that category. So, what was the 'meaning' of Pantaleo's putting Eric Garner into a chokehold? And secondly, why did Kizzy Adonis, a

---

[36] Economy and Society Vol. 1, Max Weber, University of California Press, 1978

higher-ranking black female police sergeant at the scene, not intervene to stop the killing of Mr. Garner or at least try to stop it?

If you look at the two video shoots which captured the killing of Eric Garner, you will see a black female police officer with the rank of sergeant. She stood by as a higher-ranking officer and watched the killing of Eric Garner and did not intervene to stop Pantaleo from unlawfully choking Eric Garner even though she, too, could hear Eric Garner crying out: 'I can't Breathe" eleven times. At the time, millions of African Americans wanted to know why she acted as an accomplice to the killing before and after the fact of Garner's death. Please, hold that thought. Her body language conveys meaning and therefore is qualified as 'social action' as defined by Max Weber. But what is her non-verbal body language saying?

Under the civil law of tort, no one is compelled by law to assist a stranger whose life is in danger. But officer Adonis's act of omission cannot be brushed aside as a simple instance of her being a bystander. Neither could it be brushed aside by the justice system and public scrutiny because she was sworn to enforce the law. She is entrusted by citizens to serve and protect them from harm even if a person is an arrestee or being arrested. She had a duty of due care according to police standards everywhere to rescue Eric Garner from Pantaleo's deadly chokehold. Even if doing so could cost her, her life.[37]

So, she committed an intentional act of omission under the color of her authority by choosing not to do

---

[37] Sgt. Kizzy Adonis plead guilty to failure to supervise on or about August 21, 2019. She lost 20 vacation days

her duty to protect Eric Garner from the chokehold put on him by Pantaleo and all others who with their combined body weight held Eric Garner down on the ground thereby assisting in his execution by "…compression to body and prone positioning." Mr. Garner's experience of the chokehold was that he was being suffocated to death.

Let's dig deeper into why Sgt. Adonis like other officers just stood there and watched Garner choke to death. Peter L. Berger and Thomas Luckmann argued their theory on Max Weber's definition of social action as being 'meaningful'. They argued in their book that society is not what it appears to be because what it appears to be is an imperfect mirror image of a creatively constructed virtual social reality. Everything we know, indeed our world view, is an interior virtual construction. It is not wholly exterior to us in what we call the natural environment.[38]

What happened to Sgt. Adonis happens to everyone but is more complex in African Americans. We all see through stereotypes of every form in and through our subconscious. In fact, the locus or origin of all our social acts begin in the subconscious as we first steer our way through our perceptions of things and other people through learned stereotypes of them or an even a broader world view. Even language is stereotypical code.

We participate a virtual social reality constructed with symbols and images. There are countless virtual social realities. When two or more people share symbols there is born in a moment a collective subconscious glimmering with shared meanings. Some meanings span

---

[38] Berger, Peter, Luckmann, Thomas, The Social Construction of Reality, Anchor Books, 1967

our subconscious in mere seconds like a fleeting image or sound, others in centuries like dogma, symbols, or a world view.

But let's begin first with the question where exactly was Pantaleo when he first sighted Mr. Garner and when he began to choke Mr. Garner? When Pantaleo first saw Mr. Garner, he first subconsciously participated stereotypes of black men prior to acting out the feelings he harbored for all black men and women when he met Garner that fateful day. So, you see, he formed an intent as a mental state through the stereotypes of black people in his subconscious. That is the society in which he participated in relation to black people no matter what their social status or gender may have been on that day.

No amount of police training on criminal procedure could outweigh his subconscious engagement and perceptions of Mr. Garner. Because it was not only the stereotype that he perceived Mr. Garner through but also the sentiments associated with that stereotype learned in his childhood. That is what triggered in him a burst of maliciousness targeting Mr. Garner not the cigarettes per se. Pantaleo hates black people. Garner was a black man. Therefore, Pantaleo automatically directed hate or feelings of disaffection onto Mr. Garner. But the question remains, why did Sgt. Adonis act as an accomplice to Garner's killing by placing her hands on her sides in a relaxed posture passively listening to what was being screamed out of Mr. Garner's mouth: "I can't breathe'?

Photo 1 Source: Dogon Village

Descendants of slavery suffer from a paradox of identity. One of the truisms of being a descendant of slavery is that you are always a cause of anxiety which is physically felt and expressed in some way by most Caucasians. The paradox arises for us because generally we suffer the same anxiety in relation to other descendants of slavery. Let me use an example to further explain my point.

Do you remember the movie 'Precious'? There was a scene in the movie which stood out to me as an exploration into the very subconscious of the main character, Precious. Precious was in her bathroom looking at her image reflected in the mirror (the mirror is a symbol of the subconscious). But as she looked, she saw the image of a white girl instead of her own image (the white girl image is the stereotype she perceives herself through, but which contradicts her reality as a black girl.) That scene brought out what dominated the subconscious of Sgt. Kizzy Adonis at the scene of Eric Garner's killing. It is the subconscious stereotype of far too many descendants of slavery.

Sgt. Kizzy Adonis saw herself through her subconscious which is made up of the same negative stereotypes associated with black people particularly black men as are in the white police officers' subconsciouses. She was merged collectively subconsciously with her police colleagues in those moments who shared the same meanings about what black men and women are.

For her to see herself as a white woman through her subconscious she must continually deny what is consciously self-evident to her. She must deny that she is not white. She must do that by any means necessary. In her subconscious, she is a white woman and thus her exterior reactions in real time and space to black people including herself in general are the same irrational reactions which police officers have to black people in general as they see them through their subconscious. Such mental conditions are the cause of significant psychopathology in African Americans and may explain much black-on-black homicide.[39]

For example, in the famous 1940s Baby Doll experiment done by Kenneth and Mamie Clark, black children in that experiment were given a choice to play with either a black or a white doll. Consistently, the black children chose the white doll to play with. When the children were asked why they chose the white doll the children responded that the white dolls were good, clean, pretty, and that the black dolls were ugly, dirty, and bad. In

[39] Fanon, Franz, Black Skin, White Mask; Grove Press, New York, 1952

more resent replications of the Clark experiment, the black girls chose white girl and boy dolls. What does that 'mean' (their choices are examples of Max Weber's meaningful social action theory) and what is its relevance to the black female sergeant present at the Eric Garner killing?

"The rational is real and real is rational" does not necessarily hold true in the subconscious.[40] No amount of education or rational development can overcome the onslaught of the sheer mass of negative subconscious stereotypes internalized by black children early in their lives. So black children are torn in two early in their lives. They live their lives feeling a deep idling anxiety caused by their irrational subconscious identification with whiteness and the contradictory conscious reality that they are not white.

Sgt. Adonis is like the character in the movie 'Precious'. She like Precious was looking into the mirror of her subconscious at the time of Mr. Garner's death. She found unity with her racist colleagues because she identified with them. The problem for her was and is 'reality', but the reality she wants as little to do with as possible.

Yes, she sees her reflection in the actual mirror as a black woman but overlaid with that is the subconscious image of a white women; it is the contradiction she lives every day like hundreds of millions of black women wherever white supremacy is dominate and controlling. She is either wearing blackface or delusional, so she tries to wipe the black off her face. Soap…rub hard…and more soap maybe skin bleach. And if it helps her to feel that she has wiped the black off her face, she feels that she will be in greater sync with the code of her white colleagues. Then so be it.

---

[40] Hegel, Georg Wilhelm Friedrich, The Philosophy of Right; 1820

6

You Are Monetized Slaves

The U.S. Constitution implied capitalism to be the national economic paradigm in 1790.[41] The founders were heavily influenced by the Bible (its endorsement of slavery)[42]; the Law Code of Manu (The Laws of Racial Purity), Francis Bacon's book, New Instrument, 1620; John Locke's book: 'The Second Treatise of Government', 1690; Johann Blumenbach's book: On the natural origin of Human Variety, 1776; Adam Smith's book: 'The Wealth of Nations', 1776, and Thomas Malthus' book: An Essay on the Principle of Population', 1798 and Count Joseph De Gobineau: Essays on the Inequality of Races, 1855. The founders intended to and did design the national marketplace in such a way as to monetize everyone and everything in the environment when needs, opportunities, and means arose. No one or thing was excluded from being exploitable. No real need to rush to read those books because our lives are products of the application of their ideas.

Our cry for reparations is taking place within the

---

[41] Article 1, Section 9, Clause 1
[42] Leviticus, Chapter 25:39-46

context of an economic paradigm at odds with it. Justice and capitalism are mutually exclusive ideas unless a group adopts and Aristotelian definition of separate and unequal justice. That is why I think that reparations will never be given to African Americans in the form it should be given. Most people in Congress will propose educational or job training endowments like the O.E.O. of the 1960s.[43] It obviously failed and so would a new policy like it.

I'm certain that behind closed doors the political power elite talk about and know full well that family and educational structures in the black community as well as a burgeoning black prison population would make it impossible for the majority of African Americans to reap any benefit from such a policy. The reality of the situation for many descendants of slavery is far too toxic for them to accept that as reparations.

While you've been asking for reparations, white supremacists have been doing what they always do to us. They've been fitting you into the exploitative paradigm to make you grow wealth for them. There are many ways that we have been duped into growing wealth for white supremacists. But all those ways have one thing in common. Each is predicated on our willingness to trust some of the major financial institutions, political celebrities, and people in our communities who promote those institutions and the illusions they manufacture.

The truth is that we are no different than the millions of African people who lived out their lives in past generations. They misplaced their trust, and we have

[43] Office of Economic Opportunity was set up under Lyndon B. Johnson's War on Poverty initiative in the 1960s.

misplaced our trust, too. We have been putting our trust in people who mean us absolutely no good. We are being duped, again, and it won't stop until we stop it. The truth is we have been living out our lives on a massive financial plantation. An inescapable swamp or bottomless tar pit as were thousands of black people during share cropping. We have been and are literally its slaves; we have been growing wealth in many forms for every other ethnic group but our own. We have been paying for our position at the bottom of the social hierarchy.

It's not just the money made off our bodies in private, state, and federal prisons. It's much, much deeper and more sophisticated than that; and that is exactly what 'the power elite' don't want you to know. They don't want you to know because their maintenance of your ignorance through all the channels of their media is crucial to the smooth operation of the confidence game being played on you. So, let's talk about the primary mechanisms which have been driving your monetized status. First, the Federal Reserve Bank which is like the Bank of England, and secondly, the Internal Revenue Service.

Both were instituted in the year 1913. They were instituted specifically to monetize American citizens. The Federal Reserve Bank was instituted by an act of Congress and signed into law by President Woodrow Wilson. Whereas the Internal Revenue Service was instituted by the states as the 16th Amendment to the U.S. Constitution. The Rothschild and J.P. Morgan families along with U.S. Senators and Congressmen were the forces who pushed the two forms of legislation.

You can see that when elite white supremacists want

to monetize American citizens, they can push it through Congress whereas descendants of slavery who have been demanding that Congress act to give us reparations cannot even get a Congressional bill to the floor of the house or Senate for a vote. That is because Congress does not respond to our demands for social justice. Congress responds to money making schemes engineered by A.L.E.C.[44] or by some other dominant white supremacists' group or branch of the military industrial complex.

I want to focus on what for us are two important characteristics of both the Federal Reserve Bank and IRS. Thus, I am limiting this chapter to a description of the effects on our financial quality of life for from a very little talked or written about angle. It is one of the most benign forms of exploitation ever perpetrated on descendants of slavery.

The first characteristic of the Federal Reserve Bank is what is called 'The Reserve Banking System'. The 'Reserve Banking System' is a banking method devised in Europe by early Bankers or 'Gold Smiths. And secondly, a specific law under IRS. It is United States Code 501(c)(3) non-profit tax-exempt status for non-profit religious corporations. Both the Reserve Banking System and 501(c)(3) tax exempt legal status have been and are curses on descendants of slavery.

For over 116 years, both the 'The Reserve Banking System' and 501(c)(3) non-profit religious corporations' tax-exempt status have functioned to normalize religious corruption in our communities and to push whole communities into financial sink holes trapping

---

[44] American Legislative Exchange Council

descendants of slavery in inescapable poverty throughout the United States.

It just so happens that at the same time America was industrializing at a rapid pace. Thousands of Descendants of Slaves were streaming into growing port cities. They were escaping southern Jim Crow repression and poverty. They were searching for jobs and educational opportunities. They were poor and illiterate. They were also generally very religious. So, churches catering to their emotional needs to socialize and defend themselves from racial violence perpetrated by white people sprang up by the thousands everywhere in growing urban ghettos.

The founders of the Federal Reserve Banking System have had hundreds and maybe thousands of years of recorded historical experience dealing with human greed and how to churn it. The 'Federal Reserve Banking System' allows banks to loan out 90% of church deposits if they reserve at least 10% cash on hand for daily withdrawals. Churches deposit their tithes in hundreds of banks nationwide. The tithes then become the sole property of the bank to do with as they please. Being legally enabled to loan out a depositor's money is literally giving free unearned money to banks to use to make money by earning interests on loans made with depositors' money.

The loans are generally made to businesses outside ghetto communities and so billions of dollars deposited by Churches nationwide are used. Banks rarely worked to loan to African Americans to build up their homes, businesses, education and educational facilities within their redlined districts. And to add insult to financial injury, most church leadership don't to this day even provide burial insurance for their long-time church and masjid members.

The IRS tax exempt income status attracted thousands of psychopaths, religious frauds and hustlers into church and masjid ministries across the nation. A Church was for them a place to legally *monetize* a congregation styled after the Catholic Church who did it in Medieval Europe.[45] It was a place where they could have some power, some money, and some sexual opportunities even though being functionally illiterate or trained in a white supremacist form of Christianity[46]

Each of those personality traits make for a classic definition of 'the Passion for Distinction'. They are traits rooted in our basic human instinctual insecurities and as such that passion is common among all other animals. However, preachers' passion for distinction was and is hardly a justifiable motive for them to claim that they have a 'spiritual calling'....to take money from you to give to their masters. White Supremacists bankers have been quite adept at triggering those passionate insecurities among some descendants of slavery. By doing so, they unleashed in every neighborhood across this nation irrelevant religious rivalries driven by shameless greed

---

[45] Crawford, Ashley, The Importance of Indulgences During Medieval Christianity,

"In the sixteenth-century indulgences had already taken on the characteristic of a pure money-making act ... a way of creating revenue."

[46] The American Dilemma: The Negro Problem and Modern Democracy, by Gunner Myrdal with the assistance of Richard Sterner and Arnold Rose, Happer and Row, Pub., New York and Evanston, 1944; pp. (861,862,863,866,873,874,875)

and divided along the lines of ridiculous bronze age mythologies.[47]

Thousands of preachers were very successful at instigating thought chaos. They were thus able to carve out a monetized congregation for themselves among illiterate descendants of slavery. It didn't matter to them that their own people were still in the throes of plantation ignorance. The same thought chaos persists to this day because each religious orientation must fashion, twist, and morph Bronze age myths in such a way as to differ from others.

The fact that descendants of slavery did not evolve within themselves an authentic spiritual insight and tradition set them up for social schism. Thus, they borrowed from cults, the Torah and New Testament a Hodge podge of verses centered on what was taught to them about Jesus on the slave plantations of the south. That is why nearly all preachers must deny the scientific method and evidence as the basis for doctrinal credibility or authentic spiritual insight. By denying the scientific method they were enabled to claim that they were in possession of the true religion without proof. They could, thereby, lock their monetized flock in their church for life. What they did and continue to do is spread their brands of religious franchises across black communities. But it wasn't and is not just a matter of spreading their brands of religious franchises.

What the preachers did was to instigate infinite varieties of ideological and Bronze age mythological divisions among African Americans. At the same time

---

[47] Ibid

there has been virtually no financial cooperation between different congregations and for the banks that was and is a collateral benefit. It is called 'divide and conquer'. So, instead, thousands of denominational churches competed to grow church memberships which would give them leverage to qualify for bank loans and preacher perks.

What the bankers knew is that poor individual descendants of slavery had no money to deposit in their banks in either a savings or checking account. But what they also knew is that descendants of slavery were religious and starved for a social buffer against oppression. They knew that they would tithe in church because they believed in a Bronze Age mythology to do so. For example, the verse: "A tithe of everything from the land, whether grain from the soil or fruit from the trees, belongs to the Lord; it is holy to the Lord." (Leviticus 27:30) is the literal justification used to take nickels and dimes from wretchedly poor people.

This is one of many verses which exemplify a bronze age method of extortion and fear mongering which succeeds only when people are ignorant. People not long free off the slave plantation met the qualifications to be a 'mark' for con artists. They perfectly fit the qualification after slavery. Is it their fault? No, tragically there was no one or group to protect them from lecherous people among them and to educate them.

Early on during the first half the 20th century, most churches were promoted by Prince Hall Masons or individuals who had a 'calling'. If they went onto the Masonic track most of the ministers were initiated into their network. Some knew and were willing informants for the government or agents for financial institutions while most others were ignorant of exactly what white supremacists' financial institutions were doing with church money.

In other instances, they were selfish narcissistic financial opportunists. In still other instances, they were and are just simply crazy individuals. What attracted them was the prospect of making a lot of money and gaining fame in the theatre of black drama played out in segregated America. If they serve the interests of financial systems, which they are compelled to do, no branch of the American Justice System will ever take seriously the fraud they perpetrate against illiterate and poor descendants of slavery. They would never block the revenue stream flowing out of the ghetto into their hands.

The reason is that the Income Tax Revenue Amendment of 1913, the law that implemented a federal income tax, included a provision exempting from taxation "any civic league or organization not organized for profit, but operated exclusively for the promotion of social welfare." There is no written record of the rationale behind the provision, but it is thought the Chamber of Commerce lobbied strongly for the exemption of business and civic associations (Reilly, Hull, and Braig Allen 2003)."[48]

White and Black Churches have funneled trillions of dollars into commercial banks over many decades. For example, black people donate about 17 billion dollars per year to their churches. Through our churches and Masajda we continue to pick cotton for white supremacists.

---

[48] In 1924, the statute was amended to include local associations of employees

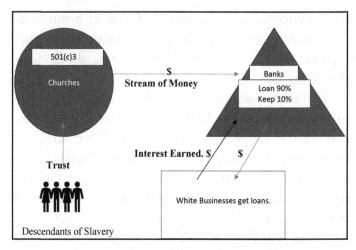

Figure 5

7

A Place in the American Pod

We reject the legally sanctioned disadvantage we suffer in America in word, spirit, and action. We assert our right to a place in the American pod. Whether it be wealth, education, family, or simply smiles reflective of a self-determined image in our minds of a future for us, we claim it as ours.

Mendel scientifically proved that the physical traits of peas are heritable from one generation to another by virtue of belonging to the same pod.[49] Unlike the pea in the pod, our status was defined to be the antithesis of 'belonging' in America's pod. Forced onto the sidelines of opportunity, benched and not allowed to play because of the color of our skin, our sojourn in the United States has been one trial by ordeal after another. We have been forced to walk backward while all others were prompted to take advantage of us to get advantage for their families. The U.S. Constitution, state laws, city and county ordinances were the rods in the spokes of our wheels bringing us down time and again. Originally, it was never meant for

---

[49] Experiments in Plant Hybridization, Johann Gregor Mendel, 1866

us to have an estate, to be in the American pod. Now it is our last chance in the waning days of the U.S. empire to stake our claim before it is too late.

We were not lied to in the beginning of this nation. We were told that we could never be in the social, economic, and political pod because the national pod was for white people only. Only they could inherit the fruits of American society we were told. We were told that we could never enjoy the fruits of American society.[50] That made it generally impossible for us to imagine or practice a life free of both contagious emotional hatred and socially constructed barriers to our personal and collective aspirations.

And now you repeat your exclusionary history of racial exclusion. You are denying our right to inherit and practice a constitutional right to choose the leadership of this nation. In dozens of states, you have passed laws to suppress our fourteenth amendment right to vote freely without intimidation and violent repression. We shall not respect such laws, ever. So, if you see lightning and hear thunder on a cloudless night, that is us coming after our stake in democracy.

Remember Freddie Gray? He was killed in 2015. He had been taken on a 'Rough Ride' in a 'paddy wagon'. I sat watching news segment after news segment which covered the aftereffects of the Baltimore riot along West North Avenue. It showed black people sweeping the streets clean of debris and except for one person, cleaning out a CVS store which had been burned and looted the day and night before. The people doing it rationalized their

---

[50] The Doctrine of Exclusion, Maryland, 1638

volunteer work by saying that they were helping to keep "their city" clean.

There are several disturbing images in that news piece. For me to know and understand that our people living on West North Avenue where the protest had occurred receive no financial return for all the money that they spend in the city lies at the heart of the problem of their disenfranchisement, their lack of an estate or stake in the fruits of American society.

As they moved to the end of their volunteer project, I could only think that something toxic remained deep at the core of Baltimore's pathways. That toxicity is such that no amount of street sweeping, paint overs, and government programs can clean away because toxic waste literally rains down constantly on the dispossessed of Baltimore. It emanates from the centers of corporate power. It is driven by its greed and by endemic political corruption both of which are a Constitutionally sanctioned way of life in America. If ever altered I think it would be the end of the American power structure. What I mean is that America is exactly what it is meant to be.

I watched individuals who were cleaning up a street on which they don't own title to any of the properties even though they and their families have lived in that area for hundreds of years. Each of them is a tenant at will, maybe at best a lessee corralled by the blurred lines of redlining, restrictive covenants, and the bright lines of poverty. And tragically what is happening simultaneously to their living space is an accelerating process of regentrification that is forcing more and more of them to bundle up their personal belongings and leave Baltimore to parts unknown.

So, here we are, completely transited out of what we might call a traditional cultural era of our history. Three to four generations of descendants of slaves are for the most part unknowingly coping with vast social and economic changes that have occurred. I don't mean the consumer consumption part of the American economy, nor do I mean here the structural system of American society. What I mean are the infrastructural ways or methods by which things are made and the lifestyles associated with the making of things. The lifestyle issues are important.

Never has the black narrative or consciousness in America been so splintered. It's as though African Americans have been blown apart. We are plagued with questions concerning how to respond to post-modernism. Whether we know it or not we don't know exactly where to go in response to it. We are forced to be reactionary instead of being active or at least preventative. Many descendants of slaves 'bend a knee' to the power elite. And even more disturbingly, most of our people cannot read the power elite's handwriting on the wall. It reads: 'Get out and stay out we want our urban spaces back.' That even though we are not given the means to get out and even if we were given the means we have nowhere to go. Ours is a dire predicament.

Deep pathos is entrenched in people all around us. We are again being assigned roles and scripts not of our own choosing just as was the case during slavery. If America's multifaceted corruption ever ebbs too low, such as the 1930s depression or the 2008 banking scandals and economic collapse, we at the bottom of the social hierarchy will suffer first and foremost as we did before.

Those times of trouble followed decades of factory closures or the exodus of capital, i.e., manufacturing companies relocating overseas out of cities like Baltimore, Maryland and Oakland, Ca. Beginning in the 1970s, it was and is the signal moment that the economic aspirations and hopes had by so many African Americans to join the middle class would be crushed. Their children would inherit nothing, but wanton militarized police violence perpetrated against them. It drove home to them the point that they don't even have a stake as a homeless person living their life out in a tent on the streets of America

Simultaneous to the exodus of capital out of the United States, white flight out of large cities and a large youthful and hopeful black baby boom population were mired in inner city concentration camp ghettos. Consequently, economic trials for African Americans have multiplied. Nevertheless, their hope in having a stake in America, to be in the pod, made them ready to vote. They experienced a child-like enthusiasm spurred on by Dr. Martin Luther King, Jr. and Malcolm X.[51] Spurred on they claimed a stake in the democratic political party process.

They voted into office black bourgeoise politicians who they hoped could usher in a new economic and policing era for them and other poor people. But little did they understand that those black bourgeoisie were never cut out to be leaders and would be hapless in the face of powerful urban white supremacists. Many of them were corrupt[52] and all of them lacked proportionate resources to

---

[51] Al Hajj Malik Ash-Shabazz

[52] Baltimore black Mayor Catherine Pugh, 69, pled guilty to Federal charges of conspiracy, tax evasion on February 21, 2019

push back against the economic and police power of urban white supremacists. The result was that black bourgeoise with all their fraternal and sorority connections could muster only flaccid symbolic responses.

I laughed to offset my feelings of frustration at having to watch the grand political theatre played out by black mayors, city council members, and preachers. I knew that they had lent themselves out to white supremacists to cast shadows on the wall to mislead black people that there was substance to their theatre when at most they were set up to perform ongoing magic tricks before their audience. There never occurred a transition from mere political symbolism to a more equitable distribution of national wealth in history.

But let me say that reality would and does continue to sink into the consciousness of black people in Baltimore or at least some of them. At the time of Freddie Gray's death, the State Attorney General was black; the mayor was black; there was a black police commissioner, a black superintendent of schools, and two-thirds of the city council members were black. Whereas ironically, Baltimore's jail was ninety percent black; sixty-one percent of high school dropouts were black; twenty five percent of the people living at or below the poverty line were black; forty-one percent of black 25-to-54-year-olds persons were unemployed; eighteen percent of homes were vacant in black neighborhoods; and out of a population of 651,154 people, fifty-nine percent of the black families are single parent female headed households. And to add insult to injury, Barak Obama called demonstrators protesting the death of Freddie Gray "criminals and thugs." He did not address the social conditions that underscore the plight of black people in Baltimore due in large part to people like him, both Democrat and Republican. He did not point out that they live in permanent economic and cultural squalor. Clearly, black politicians do not make a difference whether on the national level, state level, or city level. They are cut down politically like dry grass is cut down by a lawn mower.

We cannot claim that we were lied to. We cannot claim that our stake was stolen because the simple truth is that we never had a place in the American pod. Only reparations for Descendants of slavery can level the playing field. Thus, our only hope is that we be given reparations, even if only forty-acres and a mule on land of our choosing anywhere in the United States.

8

No Place at the Table

I need to lay the foundation for this chapter. My thesis is that there are not sufficient resources for the 140 million babies born on average every year in the world.[53] Every indicator of grain crop cultivation and fish stocks in the oceans is in negative growth. Apex castes in every society will have space. They structured their economies for that purpose. But descending the social hierarchy there will not be a plate at the dinner table for every newborn baby. We have, indeed, reached our limit to growth. Increased competition for fewer available spaces among the bottom castes in societies will translate into increased violent conflict down a disordered hierarchy. Billions of people will die and along with them will be millions of African Americans who will die prematurely in the 21st century.

What we are socially faced with is analogous to setting a dinner table with only enough chairs and plates for the 1st, 2nd, and 3rd castes. You know the game 'musical chairs.' When the bell rings everyone struggles to get a place at the table. But in this game the struggle is for the first caste to go for a chair first, then the second caste to go

---

[53] The global fertility rate is declining.

for a chair second, and finally third caste to go for a chair in that order. After that, there are no more chairs at the table. One's chance to get a place at the table diminishes with the loss of one chair at a time. It is a mathematical certainty that there are going to be a few winners and many losers. The likelihood that you will be a winner out of 139,877,000 babies born worldwide in a year is infinitesimally small.[54] If you want wealth, a University education, a vocational trade, health care, a family, to own a home, then the probability is near zero because the game is rigged against us. There is nothing you can do about it. One third of Americans will never own a home. After the 2008 recession, more than 60 percent of African Americans will never own a home.

The truth is that there are no sound logical solutions to the countless problems we face on the social horizon. People will therefore be thrown under the bus. The broad dramatic stage whereon we act out our lives was founded on patently false political ideas thousands of years ago at the advent of agriculturally based societies and may simply be an unalterable reflection of our natural and intellectual limits as a species. Most other hominids have gone extinct. Is that not the handwriting on the wall for us to read? We are victims of our own natural and intellectual limitations as are all other species of life.

The idea that some people are born to be slaves or that society is a mirror image of predator and prey relations in the wilds is illogical because we really don't socialize in the wilds. We socialize within a dimensionless virtual social reality of our own creative making. What we do when at

---

[54] In 2020, there were 139,877,000 babies born worldwide

our best or worst happens first in our minds. To ignorantly act out our drama in the 'wilds' triggers a bumper cars syndrome and in so doing adds to the aggregate social madness we suffer. The outcome is that there are more links in an already long chain of destructive decisions and behaviors which warp the fabric of our social relations and nature at large. Plato alluded to the inevitable end of illogical thinking and behavior in his allegory of the cave. He made it clear that those people who draw conclusions from false premises or 'shadows on the wall of the cave' and then act on those conclusions are doomed to ultimate social collapse.

I understand scientifically and philosophically what is driving the mass dysfunction which makes the United States a sick society. Religious myths, political corruption, and economic policy decisions and practices make national and global social dysfunction inevitable. I understand that most human beings are necessarily driven by their unconscious instincts from birth. Anxiety and sexuality dominate the field of our infantile experiences, but they also set us up for mass manipulation from the cradle to the grave. So, there is a constant endemic twist in each one of us in every generation. The issue is that far too many peoples' logical skills are not proportional to their appetites in the marketplaces of America. The misapplication of cogent reasoning in the marketplaces of America by a small power elite tightens the noose around the neck of subsequent generations until all are worn away.

Many people understand collective unconscious drives. They have worked hard to master methods of collective unconscious population manipulation for the sole purposes of economically exploiting the environment, controlling populations of people, and ruling over them militarily and politically. Despite the intelligence of the power elite, they intentionally do wrong to others for monetary profit or simply for pleasure. Aside from exploitative value, they see no inherent value in human life including their own lives.

Other people who are determined to benefit themselves at the expense of others believe in and practice mythological racism or social Darwinism. Mythological racism is usually rooted in bronze age mythologies which relegate some people to perpetually disadvantaged positions in a social hierarchy. Whether by tribal kin networks, their skin color, phenotypical characteristics, or caste outsiders are marked off for malicious discrimination. Social Darwinism is predicated on the fallacious premise that there is an absolute natural standard of fitness by means of which unfit human beings can be identified. From that premise, it is deduced that once the unfit are identified they can be efficiently eliminated thereby washing a gene pool clean and fit or by preventing inter-racial mixing.

Social Darwinists claim that there is a 'moving standard' of human fitness. They presuppose that there is a constant genetic and phenotypical maladjustment had by some people in the broader natural and social environments because of subtle changes taking place in it. In short, evolutionary change means that any given species is in a constant state of unfitness relative to its circumstances and is thus always on nature's cut list.

Socially, for example, some groups have been maliciously relegated to the bottom stratum in a society and artificially made unable to access opportunities. That is the case with descendants of slavery in the United States; it is expected that a large percentage of them would exhibit a recurring pattern of failures to adapt to economic and technological changes. Those failures are false proofs of their unfitness. It is proof of crimes against humanity. What has happened to descendants of slaves in the United State is analogous to what is happening to Dalit people living under Hinduism today. The whole environment is made toxic at every level.

Put another way, if we toxify the environment then in the same proportion the environment toxifies our bodies because our bodies are environment, too. If we are disadvantaged in that kind of action and reaction contest with nature, nature will always win in the long run because it is bigger than us. That is evidenced by nature's masterful elimination of trillions of species before us without slowing down its roll. I do not suggest that nature is personal. On the contrary, nature is very impersonal in its relation to us because nature unvaryingly operates in accordance with natural laws. Our virtual social reality can fade out because it is dependent on nature.

Some have argued the premise that human rationality is driven by human unconscious instincts not the other way around. Mythological beliefs and practices generate collective sentiment. Sentiment or emotional attachments are what holds groups together all over the world. Power elites know that. They have known how to manipulate collective sentiments down through the ages. The popular acceptance of social Darwinism has made a wide pathway for the worst kinds of demogroups to ascend to the top of our social hierarchies where decisions affecting billions of people are made. The result is now a multitiered disaster.

For example, it has become an established fact that human industries have released billions of tons of carbon dioxide and methane into the atmosphere over the last two hundred plus years. Those gases in the atmosphere are correlated with a 1-degree Celsius rise in average global temperature and changes in weather patterns over the past 100 years. Industries which polluted the atmosphere were allowed to operate even though it was reported by the Journal of Science over 100 years ago in 1896 that the release of gases caused by burning fossil fuels would cause a greenhouse effect thus making the earth surface temperature warmer.

If we assume that intelligent people who owned those industries and politicians who legally sanctioned the operation of toxic industries knew how to do a basic scientific cost/benefit analysis or a risk assessment of the long-term consequences of the greenhouse gases effect on the global environment it raises the question: why did they persist in doing what they knew would eventually cause a global ecological crisis and death to billions of people and other animals in the future?

I think the answer is simple. The economic exploitation that people suffer overlaps all societies and exists within every class or caste, ethnicity or so-called race in the world. Various forms of the system have existed throughout history. It simply underscores the fact that we have yet to find a way to vet psychopaths out of our economic and political systems or to prevent them from infiltrating our systems. Therefore, most people suffer politically from what is known as a kakistocracy. Kakistocracy means government controlled by the least qualified or most unprincipled citizens. When those kinds of people worm their way into a society's vital institutions to loot a society's wealth, that society's days are numbered. The United States is that society. There are not enough plates to go around at the table for all Americans to enjoy its decreasing resources.

9

Stunted Growth

There are two inevitable life challenges no person or group can avoid. They are the challenge to generate growth and the challenge to avoid decay. There is also a challenge for each one of us to emotionally accept that there are absolute limits to growth. Eventually, all life on earth will die. Posted all around us are increasing numbers of natural and social signs of global decline. They all signal the same message. The message is that life's powers of generation are waning. We exist within the circle of all life.

African American growth in the broadest sense of that word has been stunted for centuries beginning in colonial America and continuing throughout the history of the United States. Long ago, the weight of our stunted growth caved in on our inner selves and formed complementary stunted collective perceptions of reality, again, in the broadest sense of the meaning of reality. Generations of our children, having been forced to live out their lives in the shadow lands of America, have converted what are nightmares into social relations. Their innocent minds struggle silently to adapt to economically stunted communities. Communities full of intellectually stunted adults.

It does not take a logician to construct the perfect syllogism that proves it is more likely than not that America was designed in such a way that black people could never catch up and keep up with the status quo so that they could experience a life of free opportunity.[55] What exactly did the status quo target to stunt our growth? First and foremost, they targeted the absolute natural power of youth to reproduce offspring in families. Secondly, they targeted the ability for generations of black youth to expend work energy and drive economies in favorable environments. Thirdly, they targeted our youth's power to learn and to add to the storehouse of their communities' knowledge and practical skill sets.

In opposition to the natural human tendencies of African American youth, artificially defined limits to young peoples' growth were put in place. Such limits unrelentingly press down on them so much so that it has pressed many of them into one dimensional caricature searching for meaning in a land where we were brought

[55] Maryland Doctrine of Exclusion, 1638; "On May 10, 1740 "South Carolina Negro Act prohibited enslaved African people from growing their own food, learning to read, moving freely, assembling in groups, or earning money. It also authorized white enslavers to whip and kill enslaved Africans for being rebellious." By Post and Courier and 1834 Alabama, Georgia, Louisiana, Mississippi, North and South Carolina, and Virginia all passed anti-literacy laws. Cornelius, Janet Duitsman (1991). *When I Can Read My Title Clear: Literacy, Slavery, and Religion in the Antebellum South*. Columbia, South Carolina: University of South Carolina Press.

to literally live meaningless lives. We have lived landless rural lives and disenfranchised urban lives circumscribed by having no monetary income. There being either not enough work or no work.[56] And when we do work the fruits of our labor have been grossly inappropriate compared to the energies, we have expended to generate wealth for white people. The net result is our financial stuntedness.

Economic infrastructure in the broadest sense of that phrase has both a contracting and expanding capacity. In that regard, it is like any natural environment. When demand for needs increase beyond the capacity for an environment to supply necessary things like water, food, and space then environmental resistance to population growth forces population numbers down and maybe to extinction. Urban settings in which we have lived, both north and south, for the better part of the 20th century were generally defined as depreciation zones or places where nothing could grow for black people. Ghetto poverty is characterized historically by marginalized races and ethnic subcultures.

During the share cropping era, the resistance to our growth was debt slavery and incarceration. In the sprawling cities it was redlining, restrictive covenants, organized police violence, loss of blue-collar work, incarceration, and technological innovation.[57] At the same time white homestead landowners were rewarded with high equity in their land and homes for conforming to the rules of

---

[56] Rifkin, Jeremy, The End of Work: The Decline of the Global Labor Force and the Dawn of the Post-Market Era; C. P. Putnam's Sons, New York, 1995
[57] Ibid, pp. 75-79

redlining, restrictive covenants, organized violence against blacks, and skilled jobs. They and their heirs have profited monetarily by practicing white supremacy.

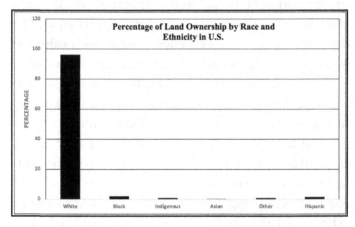

Figure 6

Those conditions have made our struggles in the marketplaces of the United States a fruitless endeavor for the vast majority of African Americans. Even when we developed thriving towns and inner-city communities during legally enforced segregation those towns were destroyed one way or another by white supremacists' county and city bureaucracies and organized violence. So, we are faced with what should be an obvious fact. There are artificially constructed limits to our growth in all marketplaces in the United States and those limits will not be lifted because the United States is in economic decline.

The marketplace of the United States can only facilitate a limited number of peoples' educational, employment, goods and services need at a given time. It has been and is a biased game of musical chairs we are forced to play; we can dart for a chair only when the chairs are all taken first by white people. Sometimes, the time frame of market capacity can be measured in days and at other times in years. No market can shrink to zero capacity, nor can any economic infrastructure have infinite linear or exponential growth. We live on the square in the mist of those fluctuations.

Combined with those marketplace fluctuations though are black peoples' natural reproduction growth patterns evidenced by us having the highest fertility rate in the United States at the turn of the 20th century. Sexuality cannot be repressed, so contraceptive methods were developed to stunt black reproduction rates. Both our birth rates and average lifespan increased the numbers of young and old African Americans in the population through the 29th century. Consequently, it increased our needs, expanded our dreams, and changed our lifestyles as we chased after what we perceived to be the 'good life'.

But at each moment of population growth, we have been met with a greater than proportionate resistance to our efforts in the marketplaces of the United States. Ever more sequestered in pockets of extreme poverty in urban ghettos like Baltimore, Maryland with all the attendant multifaceted social problems associated with that. We were stunted even more by laws which resulted in the mass incarceration of black men and women. I've wondered whether all that has happened was inevitable. I'd like to illustrate my point with a family example.

I once lived on a 288-acre farm in Mississippi during the 1950s. My grandfather had 16 children. So, counting his wife, children, and two granddaughters there were 20 persons who depended on the crop yields from the family farm for cash and food. When they matured and started families of their own, they were each given an acre or two on which to build a home when they married. Some of the sons and some of the daughters married and then built homes for themselves on the family land.

They in turn had over 8 or 9 children a piece. So, now that original 16 had become about 144 descendants of 2 persons in two generations on that 288-acre farm. By the mid 1950s, the number of grandchildren had become so numerous that it became impossible to apportion land to each grandchild. The situation had become problematic by the mid 1970s. Apportioning the land would have decreased the agricultural capacity of the farm and its gross domestic product or put another way it would have decreased the amount of crop yields, surplus produce, and cash earned each year by each family thus slowly causing each family to suffer a decline in their overall quality of life.

If those 9 children had grown to maturity and each had 5 or 6 children apiece in the early and mid 1970s, it would have amounted to about 198 persons living on the 288-acre farm. At that point it would have no longer been feasible to continue the tradition of giving direct descendants an acre because doing so would undermine the farming logistics. Combine that with an increased lifespan and care for elderly grandparents, aunts, and uncles who could no longer do manual farm work would have reduced the time needed to care for upkeep of buildings, animals, and crops.

The potential for everyone to grow on the farmland

was reduced by environmental resistance in the form of increasing scarcity of land, crops, surplus produce, and cash. More persons working the farm would not have caused a positive difference because usable land was decreasing. The law of diminishing returns was becoming evident. Our lives were beginning to become stunted by the very land that had once abundantly sustained us. We had reached the limit of our capacity to grow on it.

That is exactly what happened on the farm I lived on in the 1950s. Most of my relatives migrated to cities in the northeast and on the west coast beginning in the 1940s and 50s. There they found service, manufacturing and construction jobs. Each had between 3 and 6 children per household. Some bought homes and earned equity in those homes. Others rented. But whether they rented or bought their homes they shared a common economic loss. None of them were making, producing or growing things anymore. They didn't pay attention to that because it was so convenient to just go to the grocery store for food they once grew or raised on their own farm and besides they disdained hard farm labor even though it was their own business.

We had moved from being on the producer side of the equation to the consumer side in one generation. We had moved from growing wealth for ourselves to growing wealth once again for white businesses. We were living the illusion of prosperity in an America which was still economically segregated and harbored white supremacists' sentiments practiced through organized violence against us. The family farm of 288 acres was lost. So too are we.

All seemed to be going well for black migrants for

about two generations. But the perceived 'good health' of black people in the early 1970s was only superficial. Beneath the veneer of 'wellness', exemplified by the civil rights and cultural movements of the time, there was set in motion artificially designed benign methods of resistance to black peoples' growth. Demographically, descendants of slaves are in population decline for the first time in U.S. history.

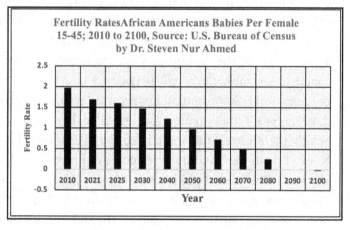

Figure 7

My perception is that black community or neighborhood degradation is set and irreversible. All of the methods I've mentioned were simultaneously employed to stunt the social growth of black people. A shrinking economic infrastructure in the form of capital exodus to foreign nations, the importation of cocaine and its offspring crack, the shredding of family structure, broken public education structures along with mass incarceration as business have the same effect on groups as a pollution, reduction of food, water, and land use in a natural environment.

Just as a population's birth and death rates decrease in a natural environment of scarcity so too are a population's social characteristics which include its birth and death rates altered by artificially designed shrinkage of economically productive infrastructures. Over time, what was once economic growth has been inverted by an artificially designed consumption cycle whereby groups become unproductive consumers. A kind of socially induced cannibalism sets in. When the body has nothing extrinsic to feed on, it feeds on itself.

10

Here, Then Not Here

Once when I thought of cities, I imagined them surrounded by industries of every kind pumping smoke out of their stacks. That was the case with the city of Oakland in the 1940s, 50s, and 60s; it was an industrial hub. Early in the mornings, union workers would stand in line to punch their timecards and on payday they would stand along a wall in long meandering lines on the way to get their paychecks. I did the same. I worked in a factory after high school.

After completing high school, I was one of the blue-collar unionized workers. I worked at the Oakland Gerber's Baby Food plant. I was as ignorant as everyone else about what was really happening to the habitat I shared with millions of other people. My youthful experience of Oakland was that of being surrounded by friends nestled in a growing and extremely youthful African American population. That community shaped my early multifaceted world view; I felt the passion and optimism of a baby-boom thrust into space and time to imagine boundless growth.

And why not? Opportunities of that time were visible and seemingly infinite, in Oakland. The civil rights movement was on track along with dozens of lesser known intellectual and artistic subcultures. I spent my weekends listening to Donald Warden (Khalid Al-Mansoor) on KDIA radio. Having dreams of a future were not difficult to conjure. Technology in the form of Harvester International's cotton-picking machine had freed many blacks from share cropping, African Americans were on their way from being 15% of the city's population in 1950 to a peak of 47% by 1980.

But reality was about to come crashing in on our celebration. Unknown to us, we had arrived for the party too late. It was really the beginning of the end, but our leaders didn't have the foresight to see it on the horizon. We were not taught anywhere to see the relation between industrialization and ecological degradation. We didn't see the high-tech revolution emerging. We didn't see the globalization of U.S. industries. My generation's window of opportunity had only lasted about 10 years.

Now, Oakland and every other city in America is severely emaciated. Industrial centers are gone. College and University costs have gone from nearly zero to exorbitant in 50 years. Student enrollment is down at least 4% statewide in California. Pharmaceutical opioid abuse is skyrocketing and so is suicide, mass shootings, and police violence against citizens.[58] And to top it off, the Coronavirus pandemic has taken as of this date over 666,000 lives and of that number 99,999 African American have died of Coronavirus. Despite that, 70% of African Americans and 70% of Latinos continue to cling to urban areas as if the economic infrastructure still had high economic absorbent capacity. Habituated

---

[58] 92,000 Opioid deaths were reported by the C.D.C. for 2020

to obsolete lifestyles and oblivious to the widening cracks in the walls of their habitat they live lifestyles which are obsolete. Everything about cities and life in cities after Americas' peak economic years has changed for the worse and so, too, has the climate and local weather patterns.

Approximately 108 billion individuals of our species have lived and died before those of us who are alive today. A study conducted by the Population Reference Bureau clearly suggest that our species will peak in the year 2040 to 2050. Then there will be an unimaginable die off. So much science has been done to drive home the point that earth is in the mist of deep and lasting changes which will challenge the very existence of the few remaining human civilizations.

In fact, we are being warned that we are in the 6th extinction. The argument concerning when life began is now replaced by the argument concerning when life will end.[59] Over 150 species of life go extinct every day or 10 percent per decade.[60] That is far more than the 49.3 which come into being per day.[61] About half of that number are insects; that is problematic in and of itself. Think of those figures as the birth and death ratio of life on earth. If you do, then you'll see that life peaked on earth long ago and is now in what is called decay. Our behaviors are describing the classic logistic growth pattern of rat populations and their social pathologies. It was demonstrated by John

---

[59] Accelerated Modern Human-induced Species Losses: Entering the Sixth Mass Extinction; Gerardo Ceballos, Paul R. Ehrlich, Anthony D. Barnosky, Andes Garcia, Robert M. Pringle and Todd M. Palmer; Science Advances, 2015

[60] United Nations Convention on Biodiversity

[61] www.researchgate.net

Calhoun in his famous experiment 'Rat Utopia'.[62] Human societies are accelerating the collapse of all ecosystems or trophic levels everywhere on earth.

The scope and magnitude of the breakdown is breathtaking. Another way to wrap our minds around the seriousness of climate change is to imagine all life forms bunched together on a single treadmill which is accelerating faster and faster so much so that each life form would need to evolve 10,000 times faster than it normally does to stay on it. That of course is impossible. Since it is impossible given present conditions, life on earth is doomed. The signs are everywhere except in the consciousness of most people.

Something we should all sense about now (2021-2022) is increasing surface temperatures everywhere. The year 2020 was the hottest year globally on record and 2021 may very well break that record. Right now, the entire western United States has been declared to be in a once every 1,200-year megadrought.[63] In California, Lake Oroville may soon shut-down because its water level is too low to generate electricity. If that happens, electrical energy supply would drop and precipitate far-reaching social consequences particularly with water treatment plants. Unparalleled heat and forest fires in California, Oregon, and Washington are destabilizing economies and the public quality of life. Lake Lopez in California is at 34% of its capacity, Nevada's Lake Mead and Arizona's Lake Powell lakes are at 36% of their capacity which is an all-

[62] Calhoun, John B., Population Density and Social Pathology; Scientific American, Inc;1962

[63] U.S. Drought Monitor; The West's Megadrought, The Week Staff, June 27, 2021

time low. Combined they are fed by the Colorado river which provides 40 million people with water.[64]

That of course means the Hoover Dam's generators are beginning to be less efficient in the production of electricity which millions of people in cities like Las Vegas depend upon. Within the next five years, the megadrought may spell disaster for the California valley from which is grown 33% of all fruits and vegetables consumed in the United States.[65] If this is beginning to describe a domino effect, it is an ecological domino effect. All our social infrastructures and natural sources of food, water, and energy describe a network of interconnected and interdependent functions. An ecological breakdown in one part of the ecosystem could cause a general social collapse.

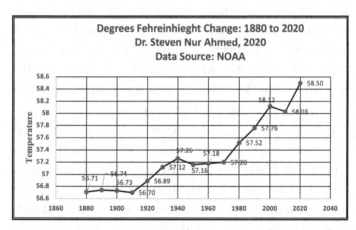

Figure 8

---

[64] The Russian River in northern California is drying up.

[65] "Over a third of the country's vegetables and two-thirds of the country's fruits and nuts are grown in California." California Department of Food and Agriculture, https://www.cdfa.ca.gov/Statistics/

That is exactly what we are facing in the second and third decade of the 21st century. To flush that out, a physicist by the name of Tim Garrett formulated a theory that 'society is a heat engine'.[66] His basic thesis is that all human cultures burn and consume wood or fossil fuels for energy to grow.[67] A byproduct of that burning is waste. Waste can take the form of CO_2 and methane when there are large densely populated cities, and an economy is based upon the burning of fossil fuels like oil and coal to release energy for use in industries which make products or for use like automobiles, jets, etc. Garrett concludes that societal collapse is inevitable[68]

The process is analogous to organic bodies which consume other life forms in a trophic level to convert

---

[66] "Central to the model is the finding that civilization's economic value or wealth, when adjusted for inflation, is linked to its rate of primary energy consumption through a constant." Tim Garrett, Professor of Atmospheric Science, University of Utah

[67] Limits to Growth, A Report for the Club of Rome's Project on the Predicament of Mankind, by Donella H. Meadows, Dennis L. Meadows, et al, 1974
This process can also be defined as the thermodynamic law 'Entropy' or the inevitable build-up of waste and breakdown of stability in systems. For a good discussion on Entropy see: Entropy: a New World View, by Jeremy Rifkin, The Viking Press, New York, 1980
See: Derrick Jensen, Lierre Keith, and Max Wilbert, Bright Green Lies; Monkish Publishing Company, New York, 2021; Solar panels will also produce waste in the form of toxic Silicon.

[68] See: Derrick Jensen, Lierre Keith, and Max Wilbert, Bright Green Lies; Monkish Book Publishing Company, New York, 2021; Solar panels will also produce waste in the form of toxic Silicon.

their energy to fuel their vitality.[69] Again, there is the wastes from organisms which are biodegradable unlike CO_2, sulfur, and methane from fossil fuels as well as chemical waste such as mercury, silicon tetrachloride, a highly toxic waste, and lead. Tim Garrett argues that there is no amount of conservation or recycling which can prevent the problem of fossil fuel and chemical waste from building up in the environment and so there is no solution to the present climate change problem. As nations' populations increase worldwide it follows necessarily that there will be more consumption and thus more waste. Some waste is biodegradable but other forms of waste will take thousands of years to degrade in the atmosphere and oceans.[70] We don't have that much time left.

We probably have reached a global average temperature of over 1.5° Celsius already. That would put the earth at 1.3 degrees Celsius more above what is called the baseline global temperature of 13.42° C (56.16° F) set in 1750. The United Nations Intergovernmental Panel on Climate Change (IPCC) concluded in 2019 that if global average temperature rises to or above the 1750 baseline to 1.5° Celsius, then we will have crossed a tipping point making for irreversible damage to our habitats.[71] Conservative estimates are presently (2021) at 1.33° Celsius due to our continued burning of fossil fuels.

---

[69] 69 Raymond L. Lindemann, The Trophic-Dynamic Aspect of Ecology; Osborn Zoological Laboratory, Yale University, ecology, Vol.23, No. 4, Octo. 1942

[70] Mann, Micheal and Lee R. Dump, Dire Predictions: Understanding Climate Change, Penguin Random House, 2008, 2015

[71] IPCC, The Special Report on Climate Change and Land; August 2019

We are trending to at most a 2° Celsius rise in global average temperature above the preindustrial baseline by 2025-30; some scientists say we are there. Any model which measures above a global average temperature of 2° Celsius is a pointless measure and can only describe how much we suffer and how quickly we die. The prognosis is tragic; the prognosis is human extinction.

Along with rising dry heat, many U.S. coastal states are experiencing increasing levels of humidity or wet-bulb temperatures. Humidity is a condition wherein the air becomes saturated with water vapor. When humidity and dry heat levels are simultaneously at and above 35°C (95°F) life threatening illness to all ages occur regardless of personal health quality because it shuts down our body's capacity to perspire or sweat. When that happens, our bodies can't tolerate it and heat builds up in our bodies causing our vital organs to fail. Heat stroke will then occur within hours killing anyone who is exposed.[72] Many human and animal habitats will become uninhabitable due to high humidity as early as 2035. Whole nations will collapse never to be revived. It has happened before[73]

Some states which are at high risk for high mortality rates due to humidity induced organ failure and heat stroke as well as forest fires are Oregon, Washington, New York, California, Alabama, Florida, Louisiana, Texas, and Mississippi. They are just some coastal states

---

[72] Raymond, Colin, Mathews, Tom, The Emergence of Heat and Humidity too Severe for Human Tolerance; Science Advance, 08 May 2020, Vol. 6, no. 19, 1838

[73] Weiss, Harvey, ed. 2017 Megadrought and Collapse: From Early Agriculture to Angkor. NY: Oxford UP

which already have high average wet-bulb and dry heat temperatures. Each of those states are where millions of poor African Americans live concentrated in urban areas. Urban habitats are heat engines in hyperdrive. Concrete absorbs and retains heat from the sun. Concrete buildings, driveways, sidewalks, and streets crisscrossing cities will become hot gridirons which can add 22°F more to temperatures already at record- breaking degrees. Cities will become mega furnaces.

Most descendants of slavery live in 17 southern states. The southern states will suffer the most and they will suffer first due to climate change. We should expect that millions of African Americans will fall victim to the recklessness of corporate polluters of land, air, and rivers. There isn't anything that can be done to stop them. African Americans should abandon coastal and urban habitats as soon as possible or face an average global temperature of about 2.3° C by 2030.

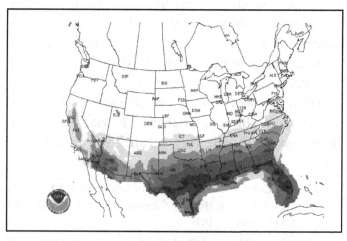

Figure 9

One other very important side effect of the social heat engine is the greenhouse effect. It occurs when the sun's radiation gets into our atmosphere but is trapped by gases in our atmosphere from being reflected out into space. Thus, greenhouse gases cause a negative feedback loop.[74] The North pole is a special case. Resent research has concluded that the arctic is warming at a rate of 13.1% per decade. That is a rate of change 4 times faster than the rest of the world.[75] For millions of years the arctic icecap has reflected sunlight off its bright surface and back into space.[76] That has prevented the deep artic water from heating up.

The albedo effect has had a cooling effect on the earth for millions of years. It has maintained the seasonal cycles, the A.M.O.C. in the northern and southern hemispheres, and a stable polar vortex and jet stream over both hemispheres.[77] But now the temperature difference between the arctic and the equatorial zone is decreasing. What is now predicted is that we are quickly climatically regressing back to a climate which existed 3 to 4 million years ago during the Pliocene era when there was no polar icecap at the north pole and the average global temperature was 7° Celsius higher than it is today. That will cause to unfold a plethora of existential challenges to mammals' survival. It was a time long before our species existed.

---

[74] Carbon dioxide, Methane, Nitrous Oxide, and synthetic fluorinated gases.

[75] https://www.cbc.ca/natureofthings/features/the-arctic-is-warming-faster-than-anywhere-else-on-the-planet

[76] The 'albedo effect' is the reflection of 90 % of radiation from the sun off ice back out into space.

[77] Atlantic Meridional Overturning Circulation

The West-Nile-Valley and zika viruses were but knocks on the door of humanity's varied habitats. The coronavirus global pandemic was the door kicked down. Such has happened many times before in human history. Whole nations have been wiped out due to bacterial viral infestation.[78] Animals are dying because their habitat niches are being destroyed by climate and weather changes. You probably don't see the direct connection between you and the deforestation of tropical rain forests and the deoxygenation of oceans and lakes. That is understandable because your world view is cluttered with corporate iconography, mythology, and falsehoods. But animals are on the move and some of them pose existential threats to human survival.

As of September 2021, over 666,000 people in the United States have died because of a coronavirus infection. African Americans, Latinos, and indigenous people have died disproportionately. The high death rate generally and specifically the disproportionate death rate for historically poor people is a sign of the horrific death rates to come due to climate change and vector borne diseases. Vectors are carriers of bacteria and viruses many of which cross over (zoonotic) into human habitats by consumption or by having contact with their blood them. Malaria is a good example of mosquito vectors causing 1-3 million deaths per year worldwide.

Corona virus deaths at 4.55 million worldwide have surpassed malarial deaths worldwide and continues to

---

[78] Snowden, Frank M; Epidemics and Society: From the Black Death To The Present; Yale University Press, 2019

rise.[79] My point here is that as animal refugees increase, we will suffer more bacterial and viral infections and deaths from once exotic and heretofore unknown diseases. Even bacteria and viruses which have lain dormant in permafrost for thousands of years are being stimulated back to life by exposure to sunlight.[80] Here in the United States, we will first see more viral and bacterial disease outbreaks in the coastal states and southern states. But no matter where we live, none of us will be able to escape harm from epidemics or pandemics.

We were not prepared for the coronavirus pandemic when it struck in late 2019 and into 2020. Our entire economy was brought to a grinding halt. All our social fault lines were revealed for the world to see. And we are still fighting variants of the virus in 2021. Now, we wait living in fear and hoping that a super variant does not evolve. But our hopes that covid-19 viral RNA stops its blind A,C,G,T recombination process means nothing to it. Because it is a virus biologically blind to the same evolutionary process that we are. Afterall, we are an evolutionary variant, too. Look at what we've done. I don't think we'll survive what's coming. The climate reversal we face is a condition which predates our existence on earth, one for which we are not adapted.

---

[79] As of September 2021
[80] http://www.bbc.com/earth/story/20170504-there-are-diseases-hidden-in-ice-and-they-are-waking-up

11

At Our Limit to Growth

Ecologists, biologists, anthropologists, and zoologists have always known there is a correlation between the capacity of a habitat and the growth rate of populations in it. By 'capacity' of the environment I mean the capacity of an environment to provide needed resources like protein, carbohydrates, food and water. By habitat I mean any place people live in dependence upon its resources. Thomas Malthus elaborated on two basic human predispositions. He identified (1) copulation, and our need for (2) food and water that increase the likelihood of population growth rates above or below a replacement level of 2.1.[81] One of the problems non-white people faces is that in our artificially constructed habitats we experience expanded or contracted resources depending upon the needs of white supremacists' elite. Unless there is a convergence of interests between them and us, we would get nothing.

African Americans have been working in artificially constructed habitats wherein they were made dependent on slave-masters from the inception of slavery in the United

---

[81] Malthus, Thomas, An Essay on the Principle of Population, 1798

States in 1619. Those labor-intensive concentration camps required minimal resources for our ancestors' upkeep. Squalid living shelters and daily minimal measures of low-quality meat and common staples were measured to reduce operation costs and increase plantation profits.

African Americans were defined as property. Minimal necessities were provided because it would benefit slave masters who wanted a cheaper means to acquire more black bodies so they could increase the amount of labor energy per slave that could be harnessed to do work or as market commodities to be sold. The pre-civil war fertility rate of black women was the basis of profitability during slavery. And if you've been thinking ahead then you probably know that Black women had a higher total fertility rate than all other ethnic women in colonial American and in the United States until just recently. But not anymore. The black female fertility rate is now lower than all other ethnic groups except Native Americans.[82] It is projected to drop to about 1.6 babies born to women between 15 and 45 in 2021 due to the Corona virus pandemic and a continued decline in the black fertility rate.

---

[82] Graph 1, Descendants of Slavery 'Age Specific Fertility Rate,' based on Center for Disease Control data 2019

Black Fertility: Descendants of Slavery	
Year	Babies Per Female 15-45
2010	**1.97**
2021	1.69
2025	1.6
2030	1.47
2040	1.23
2050	0.98
2060	0.73
2070	0.49
2080	0.25
2090	-0.003
2100	-0.025

Figure 10

After slavery, African Americans gravitated to labor intensive jobs as sharecroppers in southern states or as menial laborers in the northern states. However, because they were competing with whites for factory and government jobs and desired labor union membership, African American population reproduction became a threat.[83] And so they were attacked by economic discrimination, job discrimination, and educational discrimination. In other words, African Americans had limited access to necessary resources in all facets of life

---

[83] Eugenicist Margaret Sanger's Planned Parenthood targeted black women thru black church ministers and community leaders.

that would further an increase in their quality of life and population growth.

Urban habitats in which African Americans lived were artificially constructed or underdeveloped to limit population growth by every conceivable means. For example, lack of healthcare has always been a primary way to limit African American population reproduction because either no healthcare or poor healthcare increased the likelihood of the maternal death rate and or the infant mortality rate. It also increased the likelihood for premature death due to infection and accidents that required hospitalization or specialized medical care or medicines. And limited access to nutritious food increased the likelihood of malnutrition or stunted growth and or brain develop due to lead poisoning. Segregated communities isolated in habitats that were toxic would of course increase health maladies, birth defects, and shorten the life expectancy of African Americans even further.

We have generally been corralled into a Malthusian death camp as were the tribes Herero and Nama victims of genocide by the order of the German government in 1904-07.[84] All the conditions I have mentioned could have been avoided had the United States government kept its policy of reparations to allocate 40 acres and a mule to freed slaves. That policy could still free black people from the Malthusian death camp. But doing so would have required a 'convergence of interests' for the power elite. They have been prevented from doing that because the founders had made a constitutional contract with lower class whites that

---

[84] Totten, Samuel; Century of Genocide, Critical Essays and Eyewitness Accounts; New York, 2009

they would always be economically above 'black people'. Here racism takes precedence over economics because reparations would pour billions of dollars into the U.S. and Chinese economies.

It is incredible how devious individuals develop intricate well thought out methods for committing mass genocide. It was Thomas Malthus who designed the basic strategy for limiting poor people's population growth. It became the template for Indigenous and freed slaves in the U.S.

He said:

> "Instead of recommending cleanliness to the poor, we should encourage contrary habits. In our towns we should make the streets narrower, crowd more people into the houses, and court the return of the plague. In the country, we should build our villages near stagnant pools, and particularly encourage settlements in all marshy and unwholesome situations. But above all, we should reprobate specific remedies for ravaging diseases; and restrain those benevolent, but much mistaken men, who have thought they were doing a service to mankind by projecting schemes for the total extirpation of particular disorders."[85]

---

[85] Malthus, Thomas; An Essay on the Principle of Population, Of the Consequences of Pursuing the Opposite Mode., Book IV, Chapter V; Sixth Edition 1826

The limit to growth that is being experienced by African Americans is also combined with conditioned negative emotional sentiment that over time has reinforced low self-esteem in their children. Low self-esteem laid the basis in African American communities for different kinds of destructive behaviors ranging from murder to substance abuse and negative attitudes towards black women.[86] And the disproportionate incarceration rate of African people has negatively affected family structures and the marriage rate.[87] That in turn has been devastating to millions of black children[88]

Below, the correlation between the black incarceration and never married rates are demonstrated. Both have increased together since 1978.[89] No doubt it is a national pattern. But there is something else that is very interesting. Orlando Patterson described how England structured life for slaves in Jamaica. He states concerning unstable male and female unions "This type of association was perhaps the most common, especially among the young adult slaves." Not much has changed.

---

[86] See: The Doll Tests, Kenneth and Mamie Clark

[87] Graph 2, Descendants of Slavery Married to Never Married persons, Source U.S. Census Bureau

[88] "In 2018, black children represented 14% of the total child population but 23% of all kids in foster care." Kids Count Data Center, The Annie E. Casey Foundation

[89] Graph 3, Correlation between black incarceration rate and never married rate in California. Sources: CDRC and U.S. Census Bureau

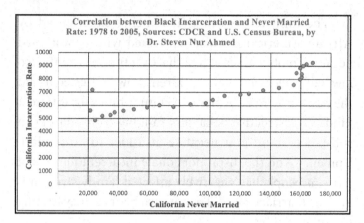

Figure 11

12

The Population Flush Cycle

The sojourn of African people in the early colonies and United States has been on an 'as needed' basis. When the need is exhausted, we will get flushed out of the United States slowly and imperceptibly by most. Those who see what is happening will be drowned out by the mass propaganda media. The founders planned it that way because they harbored an initial intent to determine immutable demographic characteristics of their new nation. It was legalized by the First Congress, Session 3, 1790, Chapter III which stated in part: "...any alien, being a free white person, who shall have resided within the limits and under the jurisdiction of the United States... may be admitted becoming a citizen." Though that law was repealed by an act of Congress on January 29, 1795, a de facto demographic policy that was driven by a collective sentimental belief in 'whites supremacists' policy continued to determine the racial composition of U.S. citizenry. However, contrary to popular beliefs racist sentiment did not originate on U.S. soil.

There was an earlier powerful European mythological driver of the founders' de jure demographic policy. That myth was and is Aryanism or white supremacy. Aryanism had started to take root in Europe as early as 16th century. It penetrated the intellectual establishment when first introduced by Vasco de Gama from the varna hierarchy of Hindu India circa 1500 a.d. Both the Protestant and Catholic churches formulated versions of it as enunciated in their policies of 'Purity of Blood', a tribal derivative of Plato's dictum on 'the importance of purity of race (Genos).'[90] Later they would adapt in whole the Hindu varna casta hierarchy in the Americas. So, in fact the founders were reflecting the current intellectual trends in racist thinking in Europe. It penetrated the collective subconscious of a virgin population; a demographic flush cycle was triggered.

Eighty percent of all immigrants into the United States were white Europeans at the turn of the 20th century. It was the largest influx of people into the United States second only to the importation of African slaves in the 17th, 18th, and 19th centuries. Such a high number of immigrants was allowed for several reasons. The first was that America's 19th century population size was too sparse to fuel its industrial revolution, and secondly to have both white workers and consumers for goods and services produced. All three had to occur simultaneously for the power elite to profit financially and to reinforce the social identity of white supremacy woven into the U.S. Constitution, state, and agency policies. What was happening in the U.S. in the late 19th century and early 20th century was a

---

[90] Plato, The Republic, [415], Plato was also influenced by knowledge of the varna system of Hinduism while he was a slave in Egypt.

population 'Push and Pull' dynamic.[91] It was also a 'flush out' of Native Americans and temporarily of Mexicans.

It was not the first time. The Irish potato famine of 1845-49 justified letting in 500,000 Irish immigrants many of whom upon arrival were compelled by poverty to join the military and fight in the Mexican American war in 1848 and then the civil war in 1861. Many of them benefited from the Oklahoma land rush for free Native American land in 1889. Later, about 4.5 million poor Irish people immigrated to the U.S. between 1920 and 1975. Ask yourself this, why didn't the Irish immigrate to Canada or Australia both of which were part of the British Empire?

Instead, many Irish immigrants took root in the northeastern cities and served as buffers against a swelling black population in those same cities. Both groups were at the bottom of the socio-economic hierarchy and were forced to compete for dangerous low paying industrial and service jobs in what has come to be called 'a split labor force'.[92] I think that white people in government took advantage of the Irish potato crisis to bolster the number of white people in the United States thereby creating another rung of a poor white trash buffer to protect the white elite. Both Irish immigrants and the white elite benefited. The losers, again, were black people. The end of the civil war did not inflate quality of life for black people. It created a nuanced array of malicious policies and acts against them.

Booming coal, iron, lumber, and oil industries

---

[91] Ravenstein, E.G; Law of Migration, Royal Statistical Society, March 17, 1885

[92] Bonacich, Edna; A Theory of Ethnic Antagonism: The Split Labor Market; *American Sociological Review.* 37 (5), October 1972

necessitated human bodies to work in them but not black bodies. But if there were black bodies, they were paid substantially lower wages for the same work done by white men or they were worked to death on prison chain gangs and sharecropping farmland in the south. The split labor market reinforced white supremacists' beliefs in illiterate immigrants. It was their reward for being white. So white families and white males immigrated to the United States and assumed employment in the growing manufacturing, city services, and military industries moving along to a middle-class lifestyle by the 1950.

The European immigrant tsunami continued to reverberate throughout the 20th century. It was white peoples' century. Whites first got economic support from the federal government during the depression years. White men and women got relief through the social security act of 1935, the minimum wage act of 1938, the welfare act of 1935, and the 'works progress administration program or WPA all under the Roosevelt 'New Deal (designed for white people)'.

After World War II, white men and women benefited from the Servicemen's Readjustment Act of 1944 or the G.I. Bill (P.L. 78-346,58 Stat. 284m). Millions of white families bought homes without suffering restrictive covenants and Redlining. Their children, not African American and Latino children, attended well-funded public schools, colleges, and Universities virtually for free. The United States was at its peak in world power and wealth. It afforded to the white supremacists' baby boomer generation an unparalleled quality of life. They are the offspring of the so-called 'Greatest Generation'.

The pattern is clear. When the power elite are thirsty, they turn the knob on and when they are satiated, they turn the knob off. Periodically and depending on social, economic, and military needs, the power elite will turn the immigration knob up or down because they perceive human bodies as natural resources usable for economic exploitation just like any other natural resource. During slavery Africans were perceived as a material resource just as oil is today. But they were not immigrants and did not fit the 'Push/Pull model defined by Ravenstein. They were not poor in Africa; there was no attraction motivating them to emigrate out of Africa. They were, however, a needed resource to drive agricultural production in the Americas. Yet, always looming in the background of white supremacists' exploitation was the high fertility rate of black women. During slavery it was of great value but afterwards it was a threat to the racial status quo. In 1910, the total fertility rate of black women was 8 babies per female between 15 and 45! That caused white elites to fear and tremble.

The population at the turn of the 20th century was getting too black to reinforce a collective subconscious national white identity. And given the high ASFR fertility rate of black people it was impossible to offset the population of black people with prevailing anti-abortion and anti-contraceptive laws. Furthermore, black people were still needed in service and agricultural labor markets. The dependence of essential markets on black labor made the power elite economically dependent on black people. So, State and Federal agencies colluded with corporations and small businesses to let millions of

Europeans immigrate into the U.S. to offset the effect of a rapidly growing dependence on the black population in the 20th century.

As quiet as it is kept, ethnic birth and fertility rates have always been political issues in the United States. Genocide was committed against indigenous tribes to reduce their populations or wipe them out; it was a federal policy. African American women had a much higher fertility rate than any other ethnic group in the United States until recently. African American females had 8 babies per female between the ages of 15 and 45 in 1900. Compared to Caucasian females' fertility rate of 4 babies per female for the same age range. Had it not been that millions of white people were immigrating into the United States, America would have become naturally racially integrated much earlier in its history without violence, Federal and State laws, and agency policies. It would have occurred naturally. A natural demographic integration was not allowed because of the demographic flush cycle.

It continues to happen. Black people are now being 'flushed' out of the demographic composition of the United States. California is a good example. It had a black population of about 7% in 1980; by 2021, the black population had dropped to about 5.78%. That is a - 0.05 rate of change over a 41-year period. In fact, the projected growth rate in 2021 is negative .01% over the next 10 years or about 134,923 black people flushed out of the California population. Some will migrate and some will die. Were it not for Los Angeles, there would be virtually no black people in California.

What are the causes of the flush of black people out

of California? We can name some of the causes: abortion, incarceration of males and increasingly females since 1980, a steady decline in the formation of families, lifestyle choices, and homelessness or poverty. I could easily segue way into many other causes, but I think the point is made. Many intersecting factors have eroded the black population in California. It is also occurring in other cities and states. Black people are being flushed out of the United States in very nuanced ways. Is it reversible? Yes, it is. The trend is highly unlikely to be reversed at this time because our labor and consumption are no longer needed for positive economic growth.

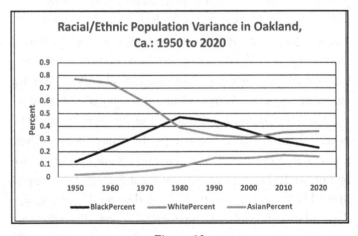

Figure 12

13

We Have No Political Power

Let's face it, African Americans are irreversibly ideologically fractured. We should not be delusional about having political power simply because some of us belong to a political party. Neither do we fit the political party mold at any level in society. Political parties are insecure by nature. They are paranoid, wandering, and ravenous groups. They feed on revenue generated by the raw energy of fear in everyday people who do political missionary work for them.

Concentrations of political power have no measurable potential to be active because political parties are either active or they don't exist. They have no cool down button, no off button. Today, none of those political characteristics apply to any black organization in the United States. Therefore, we, descendants of slaves, have no political power. Given the way we give our money away, we never will have political power.[93]

Promoting a political party or being its swing voters is

---

[93] My stomach turns whenever I think of the billion or so dollars black people gave to the Disney Corporation to see a cartoon Black Panther. It was a mental heist by Disney Corporation, and it was aided and abetted by black media and journalist who took the payoffs and screwed black people again.

not identical to the exercise of political power. Voting for the candidate of a political party is not political power. Being invited to the White House is not indicative of political power. Political philosopher Hans J. Morgenthau said: "Political power is a psychological relation between those who exercise it and those over whom it is exercised."[94] So, consistent with that premise, when Black people promote a political party, it is that party, whether Democratic, Republican, Socialist, or Communist, which exercises its power over us. For example, take the Democratic Party and Reverend Al Sharpton.

Al Sharpton was and is an intelligent charismatic influence peddler gifted with the gab. He became the heir to the 'pitch man' role for the Democratic Party after the fall of Jesse Jackson during the Clinton administration. Jesse Jackson's front organization is the 'Rain-Bow Coalition'. Sometime during the Bush II administration Sharpton assumed Jackson's role and has been front and center ever since. Now, Sharpton's full time paid job is to persuade black people with rhetorical public speeches and paid eulogies for murdered black men and women to vote in elections for various Democratic Party candidates. He is expected to steer the herd into the political corral for specific democratic candidates. Barak Obama loved him. He does a good job. He loves his job.

He has a front organization, too. It is funded by the Democratic Party and other white corporations. From

---

[94] Morgenthau, Hans J; Politics Among Nations: The Struggle for Power and Peace; Revised by Kenneth W. Thompson and W. David Clinton, McGraw Hill Higher Education, Seventh Edition, 2006

their donations he draws his non-profit salary. I know that sounds like an oxymoron; it is. The opaqueness about where his wealth derives is designed to present him as a clean grassroot leader. For instance, Al- Sharpton has no need to pander for donations on his daily WOL 1450 radio show. So, on the face of it, his show looks clean or as though he is working for the people. But in fact, he is paid for his eulogies and public speeches through his National Action Network non-profit front to which checks are written by donors and corporations. In the past, he has even promoted non-approved F.D.A. male sexual enhancement products to black males for pay on his radio show.

He is not the only one. Lesser crowd hustlers exist nationwide, but he is for now the Democratic Party's choice to be the 'Black Political King Fish'. His National Action Network is headed by local Christian preachers in large urban areas with high density black populations primarily in southern states. It's a Baptist church-based organization. It does not include Muslims, Atheists, and other black religious non-Christian groups. You must be emotionally vested in the persona of Al Sharpton to not see the chicanery of the Democratic party's script acted out through him. You must be a true believer to be in denial about it. There is no equivalent Republican black 'pitch man' in the United States for what I think are obvious reasons. Larry Elders gave it a try in California in the Gubernatorial recall election of September 14. He flopped. He argued that slave masters should be paid reparations for the loss of their black slaves.

But great things are possible. The best example of

an active grassroot political party not associated with either the Democratic or Republican parties was Black Panther Party Chairman Bobby Seale's Mayoral campaign in Oakland California in 1973. Mayoral candidates in Oakland do not run-on party platforms. Bobby Seale's mayoral campaign generated grassroot political power not 'pitch man' rhetoric. His campaign was a real surprise to the upholders of the ancient political model of what marginalized people can do politically. No other grass root political campaign had ever occurred in the United States that was based solely upon unadulterated pertinent issues. In an interview intitled: 'You Can't Drop Out of The System', published by the Iconoclast, Dallas Texas, 1973, Seale laid out his campaign strategy and policy plans for Oakland. His insight and campaign field strategy were light years ahead of every other black mayoral candidate or Mayor in the nation then and now. It was a threat to the old political model.

First, he believed that the masses of poor people could be made the majority of registered voters in cities across the nation. His campaign registered 30,000 new voters in Oakland, California. Today, we see that to be true with the ouster of 'Der Fuhrer' Donald Trump. Nevertheless, there are legislative and police efforts on the part of Georgia, Florida, Arkansas, Texas, Arizona, Michigan, Iowa, and Colorado to repress voting rights of poor Whites, Latinos and Descendants of Slavery. Their purpose is to uphold the ancient political model and to politically and economically keep us marginalized. Secondly, he had a plan to offset city budget losses due to Nixon era cutbacks to the city's OEO programs.[95] His remedy was to levy a one percent tax on intangible stocks and bonds and on Capital Gains to large corporations. Third, Seale planned to establish preventative medical health care which would have included protecting senior citizens by employing 6,700 community neighbor escorts.

Bobby Seale lost his bid to become mayor of Oakland. Redding got 77,476 votes compared to Seale's 43,719 votes. But why? Oakland's white population, driven by belief in white supremacy and by their fear and need to maintain the ancient political model, rallied to the side of John Redding. Sadly, but as usual, black churches and black bourgeoise in Oakland stood in opposition to Seale.[96] Their votes or abstentions combined with the white vote to defeat Seale. But remember, that same group of negroes opposed Dr. Martin Luther King in the 1950s and early 1960s.

A Republican, John Redding was mayor of Oakland for 12 years. At best he was a legal paper shuffler tied to corporate businesses in Oakland.[97] He was just another administrator who was in over his head like most white mayors, congresspersons, and presidents in the whole history of the United States. Seale was the antithesis of the white flacid political puppets.

---

[95] The Office of Economic Opportunity (OEO) coordinated Job Corps; Neighbor-hood Youth Corps; work training and study, and Head Start programs under the Johnson Administration but was cut by the Nixon administration in his attempt to decrease federal spending except of course for the Vietnam war military budget.

[96] Self, Robert O., American Babylon; Princeton University Press, 2003, p.p.307

[97] Ibid, p.p. 305

Seale's ideas were advanced for that time in Oakland. He criticized other black mayors like Richard G. Hatcher in Gary Indiana for being organizationally incompetent. The time was not seized. Political and economic opportunities for black and poor people in Oakland had been lost.

When Oaklanders finally did get black mayors after John Redding, they got three democratic puppets. An ex-judge and paper shuffler named Lionel Wilson, a flacid Elihu Harris, and a burned-out Ronald Dellums who was completely ensconced within the Clinton's regime. Not surprisingly, all three black mayors were elected to office having rode the wave of a young and growing black population which did not peak until the 1980s-1990s.

All most fifty years after Seale's run for mayor of Oakland, in every major city like Gary, Indiana black populations have been in a downward spiral going from bad to worse. In cities across the nation, whether it be homelessness, crime, poverty, unemployment, or the disappearance of families the evidence supports the claim Bobby Seale made about social problems in 1973.

The U.S. constitution legally and politically multi-polarized the nation based on race, gender, ethnic, and religious mythologies. The founders intended it to always be that way. The founders did not intend to politically impower all the people. They were not really for democracy then nor today. Like Aristotle, they believed it to ludicrous to allow the majority to rule the nation. Citizenship was limited to white persons how owned land. They made it clear time and again that their intention was to keep specified groups politically disempowered. The nation has always been divided by law not united by law. And what is now a national crisis of a fractured United States has always been enforced by State or Federal police violence.

Now, the United States is de facto politically multi-polarized. But the ancient myths are dying or dead and there are none to replace them. Young people just don't believe them anymore. There is no reason to believe them because they are lies. And so, every effort to be more politically inclusive is an effort to advance national unity at the expense of what we know historically to have been social divisiveness and police violence based upon political mythology.

The current resurgence of the ancient political model is driven by irrational mythological political motives. It will no doubt lead to an outcome equal to the outcome it led to in 1861 a bloody civil war and the demotion of the United States to a second-tier world power never to rise to the highest rung of international power and influence again.

14

Pragmatic Politics

The history of groups taken out of their homeland and enslaved by empires tells a repeating tragedy with no exception. It is that at no time in written history have a people taken out of their homeland and made into slaves by an empire then forced to live on the soil of the empire had a happy ending. Either by assimilation, acculturation or benign genocide such populations disappear from the pages of history. They go extinct. The future looks bleak for Descendants of Slaves in the United States.

Descendants of slaves cannot assimilate into the American 'mainstream' because the United States is based upon the premise of white supremacy. Some people think that having blended children will eradicate white supremacy. That is wrong because all one need do is look at south American nations. Each of them from Mexico to Argentina were predicated on the varna casta hierarchy. It persists to this day. If the dominant caste defines itself as white and keeps all the wealth we are automatically marginalized as non-white. Nor can we acculturate because the languages, religions, culinary habits, and dress styles we had prior to our enslavement were destroyed on slave plantations. Thus, we are left a naked lump of flesh laid out in the sun to rot. Our dignity taken, we are mocked and in turn mock ourselves. We will never know our family names.

The United States grew out of the British empire into a new empire. It is a global empire today. It is highly unlikely that descendants of slaves will give birth to an authentic culture of their own because the time has run out. Therefore, there is no reason to think that they will fare better than other groups which have suffered similar tragic experiences in the annuals of history. Of course, we are all in the same boat with a thousand holes in its hull. I accept reality without fear. But should I be hopeful?

Will descendants of slavery ever learn to be politically pragmatic? All my adult life I have watched descendants of slavery fall victim to one political fiasco after another. I can see that we have not known or have failed to learn that politics is a pragmatic relation to a population. The two major political parties haven't delivered what we've needed most. What we've needed most was not the so-call first black president. What we've needed most since the post-civil war reconstruction era is monetary damages or 40 acres of land and a mule from the U.S. government as compensation for the profits it made off our black bodies since its founding to the end of the civil war. Yes, our black bodies. We are literally an organic extension of every slave who ever lived in the United States. We are they. They still live.

We have supported presidents from Abraham Lincoln to Joe Biden. We have supported republicans and we have supported democrats. Every presidential election renews our hope and effort to get social justice. We have supported black mayors both male and female only to see our quality of life fall further and further behind that of immigrant ethnic groups.[98] What we generally fail to see is the artistry of white politics. The campaigns for our votes are fashioned to be rhetorical advertisements employing benign manipulation. They are tailored to appeal to our collective sentiments and fears. We are always told to choose the lesser of two evils. To hell with that.

I do not believe the democratic nor republican parties will ever pass a bill that gets signed into law by a president to give cash reparations to descendants of slaves. The example of the hour is H.R. 40. It was submitted over thirty years ago by x-congressman John Conyers. It is a toothless request to the judiciary committee that slavery be studied. Studied? Again? Furthermore, the proposed bill does not request monetary damages. As of now it has been passed through the judiciary committee to be presented to the house of representatives but, is being held by Nancy Pelosi because it does not stand a chance at passing in the Senate and maybe the House of Representatives.[99]

The expectation is that some democrats will vote against it. I believe that to be true because both the democratic and republican parties are at root white supremacists' institutions which serve the interests of white businesses. The absurdity of requesting a study of what the institution of slavery did to people of African descent in a nation with more than 5,300 colleges and

---

[98] There have been 32 black mayors since 1868, https://en.wikipedia.org/wiki/List_of_first_African-American_mayors

[99] As of June 14, 2021

universities each with a history and sociology departments full of published scholars is like throwing feces in the faces of black people.

We've got to kick the ideology addiction. A ready-made world view is not practical because a group's world view grows out of a population's collective experiences solving their practical problems. Since the turn of the 20th century millions of African Americans have sought to find meaningful identities in ideology and mythology. Their searches have led them without exception from one dead end to another dead end minus their money. There are hundreds of ideologies and for every one of them you will find African Americans internalizing them to frame their political world view.

Capitalism, socialism, communism, feminism, Pan Africanism, Garveyism are but a few. But you name it, and you'll find an African American who identifies with it. Sometimes, an ideology is assumed out of a sense of wanting to identify with and be accepted by elite whites. Sometimes it's the result of peer pressure and a desire to belong to a high-status group that requires people to conform to an ideology or mythology. Sometimes it's out of sheer ignorance. But few African Americans can step back out of the box and see the divisive political effect that so many political ideological identities have had on getting us out of the economic sink hole most of us occupy.

I remember listening to Kwame Ture speak. He would always shout at the end of his speech 'Organize!'[100] But he never laid out a detail strategy for African Americans to organize at the local level. He is a good example of

---

[100] Stokely Carmichael

an ideologue or rhetorician. The truth is he didn't know how to organize. For that reason, he was a half-baked socialist. Political pragmatists are not ideologues. Political pragmatists are tool users. Pragmatic activists base their political orientation upon the scientific method not upon ideology rather on praxis not on categorical stagnation. It operates on three broad assumptions. One assumption is that mass consciousness objectively exists as a characteristic of a given population and is reciprocated more or less in the consciousness of any given individual member of it. The second assumption is that population is independent of any individual in it. The population exist before each member in time and the population will exist after each member in time. The third assumption is that close observation of population movements can reveal repeating (unalterable) population patterns and thus uncover causes and correlations of repeating population patterns.

Political pragmatists proceed politically on those three assumptions. They know that participant observation and mathematical description of the characteristics of any given population and its habitats is procedurally first and foremost to any successful campaign. They ask: Where are they now? What are they now? When is it they are now? How are they being where they are now? What are the others in relation to them now? What do they need now? How can we get for them what they need now? Those are political questions. No political success can be had without methodically answering those questions. The caveat for us is this: political outcomes are binomial in nature, you either succeed or you fail to achieve your political objectives. In extreme scenarios like climate change it can mean the difference between life and death.

Political pragmatists explain what they have described. Is what has been described true or false? For over a hundred years, African Americans have hung their hats on the promises or platitudes of white politicians in both the democratic and republican parties. That was not logical. The results of coasting on white platitudes even if through a black mouthpiece has led to one unmitigated political failure after another. The campaign of Barak Obama is a case in point. Obama continually used the slogan: "Yes We Can". His campaign slogan was meant to be purely rhetorical and was aimed at arousing sentimental support from descendants of slavery without filling in the blanks 'who are 'We'? and 'Can do what' and 'for whom'? As it turns out 'We" was Wall Street and the military industrial complex and 'Can do what for whom' turned out to be maintain the status quo.

Descendants of slaves were left with a sour taste in their mouths after eight years of the Obama administration because what was and is most important for them is reparations and because reparations were denounced by him as he turned to face white supremacists once he was in office. The whole Obama presidential fiasco points to the illogical or emotional support given to Barak Obama by black people. Black people were not politically pragmatic in their relationship with Barak Obama. Black people are not pragmatic. All the fraternities and sororities or so-called educated black people acted like fools religiously supporting him.

The same had been happening in the later 20th century until mass protests lead by political pragmatist Dr. Martin

Luther King and Malcolm X, and others applied mass pressure on Federal agencies and Congress to enact civil rights laws on top of civil rights laws which had already been amended to the U.S. Constitution after the civil war. The legal redundancy was necessary because of the relapse of white people back into legalized white supremacists' discrimination through state laws and policies against descendants of slaves. History is repeating itself right now in some states only this time the situation is worse.[101] We've got to become politically pragmatic if we are going to upgrade our quality of life in America.

Political pragmatists evaluate the dynamics of a population because populations have many overlapping functions. Thus, care must be taken to identify the most important functions on a ratio scale of urgency or importance. Beginning locally where people live is the best starting point to identify what policies are needed to solve problems faced by descendants of slaves because they are directly affected by local problems. Those who do evaluation work must have no party affiliation nor be paid professionals. They must have lived in the neighborhood for a period and have children. By preventing professionals from doing local problem evaluations the likelihood of cooptation and corruption would be decreased or even eradicated.

Pragmatic political activists act to make social change through populations they participate not to promulgate or make ideological converts of individuals in populations. They work with everyone in a shared population to

---

[101] https://www.brennancenter.org/our-work/research-reports/voting-laws-roundup-may-2021

solve shared problems. The national political arena is far greater in mass than we have resources help except with a vote. But often the power of our vote in this oligarchic political system is infinitesimally too small to induce political changes we need. A case in point is the Bush v. Gore election (2000) was decided by the U.S. Supreme Court not the votes of thousands of African Americans in Florida.[102] We should do politics first locally where we can exercise power in proportion to our capacity. Then slowly build up to participate independently in state and federal arenas.

The scientific method is the only means which political pragmatists employ. Political pragmatists are simultaneously expressive and instrumental because they define the issues before councils of government and apply the tools necessary to induce equitable change or they file lawsuits. Political pragmatists do statistical forecasts based upon their description, explanation, and evaluation of population situations. Political pragmatists magnify their population's issues and expand their political power to guide the formulation of agency policies and eventually state and federal legislation and policy formulation. Political pragmatists know that if a tool is broken it must be replaced with a tool which works. A too which works in their interests. When they turn the rachet handle, they want to hear it click

---

[102] Gore, 531 U.S. 98 (2000)

15

Do You Know It's Happening?
When It's Happening

I believe that history is a modern science. Scientific inquiry is driven to inferences only by empirical evidence. Historians who employ the empirical method proceed in their field to gather forensic and authentic documentary facts as would an investigator at the scene of a crime or an attorney fighting a case in court. Those who don't apply that method are not historians. They are mythologists.

Mythologists are not historians. No evidence is admissible as a true representation of history based on hearsay or presupposition. At this crucial point in our sojourn in America, those who consider history must decide whether they will be empirical or mythological. Descendants of slavery are sensitive to this issue because it is mythology which was used to rationalize our slavery. Mythology could not be used to liberate us 244 years ago and it cannot liberate us now. It can only give to us false hope. It can only further the exploitation of us all.

I say our slavery because we who are alive are the literal organic extension through space and time of every slave who ever lived during legalized slavery in the United States.

The science of Black History and the month in which it is remembered should not just be about remembering our past experiences in the United States. Rather, Black History Month should include time for us to model our future. It should be a time to critically assail whitewashing and false representations of our history. It should be a time to identify, evaluate and explain historical patterns which can enable us to construct reliable models about the direction in which we as a people are moving in the United States and the world. When I look at what black students are studying if they do go to University or College I can see that we are not prepared enough to do those tasks in our communities.

What could be our individual and collective future necessarily grows out of what has happened to us in the past and what is happening to us in the moment 'now'. That is a simple equation. The sum of the past and present equals a new combination of personal and collective conditions. We call that our potential vital future. I think that our collective vitality is important. Collective vitality is a measurable quantity. Two examples are total fertility rate and our life expectancy.

In 2021, the Center for Disease Control reported that life expectancy for American descendants of slavery has dropped 2.7 years from January to June 2020 due to the coronavirus death rate. The corona virus death rate for descendants of slavery is estimated to be 99,999 deaths through September 2021. The actual figure is no doubt higher because many states disregarded identifying race on their death data sheets early during the pandemic. Put into perspective, it means that about 99,999 descendants of slavery died in less than two years. No doubt it will be higher when we get the C.D.C. reports for July through December of 2020. Generally, what that means is that our collective life chances and quality of life have fallen into a life sink hole.

That decrease in life expectancy is correlated with a decrease in the total fertility rate of African American descendants of slavery. Our vital signs as a people in the loosest sense of that term are growing weaker by the year. There are definite reasons for that. But the seeds to unlock the reasons are in our history and it will take scientific historians to uncover those reasons.

First, we aren't having as many babies as in past generations. In other words, as discussed in the biological sciences our population is experiencing a pattern of population decay. There is no nice why to cosmeticize it. Presently the total fertility rate for descendants of slaves in the United States is 1.7 babies born for women between 15 and 45 years of age. What that means is that the African American population in the United States is below the fertility rate necessary to replace or maintain the present population so that it remains constant over time.

The replacement fertility rate for any population is 2.1 babies born per female between 15 and 45 years of age. In other words, each year the number of African Americans in the United States will decrease by a percent, if the total fertility rate remains at 1.7 or dips lower.

Think of it this way. If you have $100 in a bank account and after 1 year 10% of that $100 is subtracted from it as negative interest, then it will leave you 90.00 dollars, then 10% from it in another year will leave you 81.00, and then 10% is subtracted from it again leaving you 72.9 and so forth. You can see that without making a deposit of 10% into your account balance every year you will have fewer and fewer dollars until overtime you reach 0 even if the negative interest remains 10%.

Population decay follows that same mathematical model. If we do not reproduce enough babies to replace the parents that sired them, then the population inevitably reduces overtime to zero. And that my dear people is where we are headed. But there's more.

There are other social indicators besides the total fertility rate. There is the COVID-19 pandemic and its high African American mortality rate at about 99,999, a rate that 15% of the total deaths or 3x that for white Americans. And finally, young African Americans are choosing not to marry for a multiplicity of reasons. The marriage rate is a strong indicator of community stability and upon which we can estimate the birth rate and the total fertility rate to be in the future. Thus, if fewer African Americans form stable families, then logically, we should expect that the birth rate will decline and of course with it the total fertility rate.

In 1945, 65% of all African American adult males and females were married. The age at first marriage remained constant through the 40s and 50s and 60s at about 20 - 22 years of age. This year, 2021, the average age of first marriage is 30 years of age for African American females. While the overall marriage rate hovers at around 23% of all African American adults. Now that 23% compared to

65% in 1940 clearly indicates a huge drop and a definite change in our perception of the value of marriage and what family is historically defined to be. These models are important.

Mathematically, we can forecast what the marriage rate will be in 2035 to 2050. For instance, in 2025 given the present rate of decline it will be approximately 17% and by 2050 the marriage rate will be approximately 14%. At that time, we can say with high degree of cogency that marriage amongst African Americans in the United States will be virtually a thing of the past and along with that a continually declining birth rate, lower life expectancy, and an increasing death rate would point to extinction.

Recently, during Black History month, I listened to a talk by a professor of political science at the University of San Francisco. His name is James Taylor. He was speaking on a popular radio station in D.C. WOL's the Carl Nelson show. He said that by 2050 there will be 70 million African Americans in the United States. That was a ridiculous claim given current population trends in the African American population. Professor Taylor didn't cite any sources for that figure, nor did he provide a statistical analysis or model of his own. I think he was being emotionally rhetorical; but he was nevertheless misrepresenting the facts.

There will not be 70 million African Americans in the United States in 2050. The truth is that there is a greater the 50 percent chance that there won't be any African Americans in the U.S. by 2050. And even if there is there is no possible way that our population will grow given its 1.7 total fertility rate and declining marriage rate. For a robust population growth to happen, there would have to be a mass increase in immigration of African people out of Africa into the United States. Of course, that will not happen because of powerful white supremacist ideologues in Congress and in state legislatures.

I have provided you with my calculations in this talk. I provided you with my forecast of the marriage rate which is a rate that represents the formation of families up through 2050. There are also other underlying economic reasons for our population decline. The abortion rate that dates to the early 1970s is a factor in the population decline of African Americans in the United States as well.

But suffice it to say that black history's greater value than just remembering what happened in the past is the construction of futuristic models which can be used to demonstrate what we should expect in the future. We should take heed because one other titanic over arcing problem we face along with everyone else on this earth is the problem of climate change.

The extreme weather patterns brought on by climate change is happening in the Pacific Northwest, Texas, throughout the Midwest, and soon over the East Coast of the U.S. It is an example of yet another extreme challenge to our lives. We are not prepared emotionally for how devastating it will be just as has been the case with the social consequences of Covid-19 and the Delta Variant.

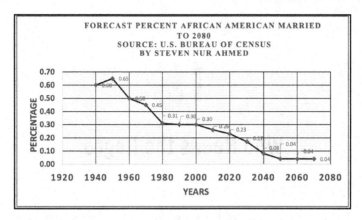

Figure 13

16

"Who Needs the Negro"

I think that some old books should be dusted off and reread periodically because they contain timeless truths which glow as brightly as they did when first expressed. They are rare and no doubt originate through a silent but laborious process not unlike birthing a child. A timeless truth is not brought into being by fiat but is a synthesis of countless other prior musings and data analyses finally coming together into something rare and unique.

Such a book I discovered decades ago. It is intitled 'Who Needs the Negro' and published by Sidney M. Wilhelm in 1971. It was at a time when its basic premise was not at the forefront of black intellectual discussions and civil rights speeches. It was overlooked or dismissed. Black intellectuals often overlook insights and lack needed foresight because they are in the moment men and women ambitiously attempting to climb as many rungs on the latter of material success white supremacists offer to them as hush endowments. You see, it's not the teeming masses of black folk that was central to their interests. No, it was Jessie Jackson's Rainbow Collation or Andrew Young's Ambassadorship to the United Nations, amid countless mayoral titles black intellectuals were granted, and paper shuffling positions which black intellectuals were really interested in. In short, they were too self-serving to be grass root leaders for the black masses. They dismissed the insight offered by others and instead pandered false hope to desperate descendants of slavery.

One of Wilhelm's theses is that: "Negroes may enjoy equality insofar as they are first made economically irrelevant."[103] Did African Americans finally achieve political equality under the law only to witness the simultaneous erosion of the very jobs they fled the Jim Crow south to access over the past seventy-years? Did we fail to be cognizant of the historical competition between workers their unions and corporations? Did we not see the hurried pace of technological changes taking place especially in the high-tech industries and manufacturing? Did we fail to foresee the exodus of capital as a reaction to unionization, corporate taxation, and increases in workers' wages? I've learned that hindsight is 20/20. Now we can see our mistakes clearly. As we look back, we may wonder why we could not seize those timeless truths before our losses mounted up and now have come to overwhelm us.

Wilhelm observed that most African Americans came out of a work tradition of manual labor. That was not a new observation and probably was the lived experience for most descendants of slaves. Gunner Myrdal had described the same labor history of descendants of slaves

---

[103] Wilhelm, Sidney W.; Who Needs the Negro? Doubleday & Company; Garden City, New York, 1971, p. 265

as did W. E. B. Dubois.[104] But what Wilhelm could see and did describe was that each economic phase from agriculturally intensive labor to manufacturing labor and now the high tech robotic assembling processes was an economic movement, spanning centuries, out of the United States. Simple reasons explain it.

I think it was because capitalists' enterprises had to shake off labor unions and as usual always seek out new and cheaper human resources to exploit at low costs. This time manufacturing companies moved to East Asia minus Japan and North Korea. The incredible thing is that 55% of Americans who own shares in U.S. corporations are just fine with crashing the United States population to all time low standards of living which amounts to deserting 45% of their compatriots.

In the past it could not be perceived that way. Asians and Africans were excluded from citizenship and were understood to be just subhuman energy resources.[105] Mexicans were promised citizenship after the Mexican American war of 1848 but were treated as second class citizens and relegated to exploitable farm laborers after that war ended. So, corporate owners did not have to suffer the pangs of guilt prior to the mid 20th century. Each group at some stage in American economic history were useful laborers and consumers. Now, descendants

---

[104] Gunner Myrdal; An American Dilemma: The Negro Problem and Modern Democracy; Happer and Row pub., 1944; Dubois, W.E.B., Black Reconstruction in America, 1860 to 1880: pub. 1935
[105] African Slaves became citizens by law with the passage of the 14th amendment. The Magnuson Act of 1943 allowed Chinese Americans to become naturalized citizens.

of slaves, having not made the transition from manual laborer to educated specialists in large enough numbers are perceived as an unproductive consumer and a national security threat because of their growing social discontent and aggressive reaction to white supremacist police repression.

Wilhelm observed that as the urban African American population grew by 86% between 1954 and 1966 it paralleled a 50% growth of industrial and mercantile construction outside the core city. The unskilled jobs were taken out of the urban center where African Americans lived. This shift was a national phenomenon. For example, it happened in Los Angeles and Oakland California. Between 1950 and 1960, 100,000 white people moved out of Oakland to surrounding suburbs. In Los Angeles, whites fled Compton. By the late 1970s manufacturing companies were also moving out of Los Angeles and Oakland. It was by design. Middle class manufacturing jobs were denied black people. It reminds me once again of the 1638 state Maryland, Virginia 'Doctrine of Exclusion' which stated in part that no black person was to ever enjoy the fruits of American Society.

Wilhelm wrote in his book that just when civil rights laws were enacted by Congress or by a Supreme Court ruling university standards for entry into their schools was elevated. For example, prior to 1968 entrance exams was no SAT test requirement for application into the University of California. Grade point average was the major criterion.

The pattern is clear to me. As the first wave of baby boomers started graduating from high school in themed and late 1960s, the SAT tests was introduced to reduce the chances for minorities to enter colleges and universities. The same method is was proposed in 2013-14 to make the General Education Test more difficult. Doing so would affect ethnic minority chances to overcome failed high school experiences. More African Americans will fail to pass the G.E.D. test because of their pervasive weakness in mathematics. Push back against advancement of minorities' opportunities is constant.

There is yet another problem. It is the narrative of leadership. Civil rights laws are not the only issues facing African Americans. Other issues over which governments exercise no control exists. A major one is automation and the inability of millions of African Americans to retool their skills to compete within the post-industrial milieu. There has been a devastating collateral effect. Liberal democrats will not speak publicly of the issue while racist extremists and right-wing Republicans like followers of Donald Trump push aggressively for privatization of state and Federal agencies like the U.S. Post Office and Social Security.

Anyone who studies the U.S. Labor Department statistics will see the real issue of the day. There are 73 million unskilled workers in the job market. Of the number 4.5 million are African American. They have the lowest paying jobs along with Latinos. Their family structures are more unstable than any other ethnic group in the United States. Wilhelm states that African Americans are those who are increasingly being made 'unnecessary' in post-industrial American labor force. But the economic system is a multi-headed beast.

What Wilhelm did not see is that a last-ditch effort would be made to make the Negro economically necessary. First, unskilled laborers would find a new place to function as profit drivers. Their role would increasingly become that of inmate in the prison industrial complex and out of prison as parolee or probationers.

The two million or more of them would enable politicians to rationalize arguments for increased taxation on citizens to keep America safe. So, inmates, even though sitting idly in their cells on new slave plantations like city jails or state and Federal prisons, would drive the militarization of police departments nationwide and indeed drive profits for whole government and private prison 'industries'. Most of them would remain profit drivers for prisons their entire lives as parole or probation violators. But it didn't stop there.

The Negro's transformation into a post-modern kind of economic necessity would manifest also in form of Bill Clinton's experiment to institute 'Workfare'.[106] Instead of benefiting mothers with dependent children, it funneled millions of tax dollars to supposed private small business employers. There was no need to trained or skilled to be in the program. Just showing up for 'work' made unemployed mothers 'economically necessary' again just

---

[106] "In 1996, after constructing two welfare reform bills that were vetoed by President Clinton,[18] Gingrich and his supporters pushed for the passage of the Personal Responsibility and Work Opportunity Reconciliation Act (PRWORA), a bill aimed at substantially reconstructing the welfare system. Authored by Rep. John Kasich, the act gave state governments more autonomy over welfare delivery, while also reducing the federal government's responsibilities." Wikipedia

as their ancestors were necessary as 'pickers' on slave plantations. But all the political subterfuge could not get past one insurmountable obstacle. It is the population decline of African Americans over the next forty-six ears. Thus, the general thesis that African Americans have become economically unnecessary remains cogent.

Sidney Wilhelm ends his book with a very foreboding existential prediction. He states: "Under the economy of past technological configurations, it was incumbent upon White America to balance racial values against economic incentives. But with the introduction of automation.[107] that necessity of virtually disappears since it is economically feasible to negate the traditional rational for the Negro's existence...the affected Negroes will not be so much abused as ignored. There will be no necessity to maintain measure of intimidation for purposes of economic returns as the Negro shifts from the economies of exploitation to the economics of uselessness.[108] And later he states: "It is the double curse flung upon the Negro by White America to judge competency against the performance of a machine and the person by the color of their skin."[109]

---

[107] 60 Minutes, Business Use More Automation, Fewer Workers, July 21, 2011, by Kelly Cobiella, CBS News
[108] Wilhelm, Sidney W, Who Needs the Negro, Doubleday & Company, Inc., Garden City, New York, 1971, p. 223
[109] Ibid pp.265

17

Pandemonium

I am suspicious of black talk radio media as well as many black YouTube channels because I know that money drives the whole media system not principle. I think that most of them are appendages to the F.B.I. national propaganda apparatus. I think some black talk radio media are paid 'cointelpro' agents just as was the case in the 1960s. They are paid to ease drop for the F.B.I. on what black people are thinking, to omit information, to misinform us or divert our attention away from serious social justice and institutional issues to ridiculous entertainment and lifestyle product promotions. Black talk radio is a microcosm of the whole media and entertainment system. It is defined by the same profit objectives. It is pro money; that is all.

I remember before the Walt Disney movie Black Panther was released to theaters, some talk radio stations avidly daily promoted the movie for hours a day. And after its release the same radio stations generated a circus atmosphere of wild call-in talk about the movie's characters and a phantasy African nation called Wakanda as though they exist. The movie grossed nearly 1 billion dollars. Most of that money was vacuumed out of poor African American communities nationwide. I'm sure the black owners of those black media were paid by the historically racist Walt Disney Corporation. No, I don't have copies of the checks given to them.

Most of the discussions I've listened to pretty much revolve around issues that are the same issues hashed over fifty years ago by baby boomers and their parents. The pattern is clear to me. For example, listen to some old episodes of 'Tony Brown's Journal' which aired from 1978 to 2008. You'll hear discussions on black history, reparations, police use of excessive force, lack of black businesses and money, ideology, politics, black poverty, chronic problems in black male and female relationships, black history, black psychology, crime, sports, entertainment, comedy, astrology, herbal treatments, and poverty all by a litany of laypersons, scholars, self-proclaimed religious and political leaders.

Current science issues like climate change are pretty much never discussed on black talk radio programs because such discussions would necessarily branch into the oil industries' abuse of ecosystems. That might also cause stations to loss advertising dollars from subsidiaries of oil companies. What more compelling evidence is needed to conclude that we have been artificially made 'caste stagnant' since the mid 1970s by many black people.

Listening to black talk radio and listening to and watching black YouTube channels is like being forced to listen to a scratching skipping-repeating record recording play repeatedly. I do not mean that those issues are not important because I understand that our social problems have not changed in 100 years. But today we are faced with a quintessential existential problem. We are in the sixth extinction.[110] Its real. Its irreversible. And, if we do not take an adaptive posture to it then we will die as a group. That means black people will die first in the United States.

For me what is not discussed on black talk shows is disturbing; what is not discussed is far more informative than what is discussed. In fact, the absence of sober discussions on global climate change and the radically changing characteristics of the black population like our dropping fertility rate and Covid-19 death rate are so extreme that I think there must be a policy of silence by owners of black talk radio stations to suppress data. I can think of only a few reasons for such a policy. They are all money and political correctness. We are in the fog of a world view paradigm shift, but you wouldn't know it listening to black talk radio.

If it is true that there is an enforced policy of silence not to discuss certain issues facing black people, then it is either because listening audiences are completely uninterested in the issues of climate change and population decay. Or they are ignorant of those issues. Or the owners of black talk media have been told by government agencies not to make the issue of climate change and black population changes

---

[110] Ceballos, Gerardo; Accelerated modern human–induced species losses: Entering the sixth mass extinction, Journal Science Advances, 2015

a topic for their shows.[111] The threat is that if they do then they will be defunded.

I think that not revealing the raw data to encourage free sober discussions on a broad range of issues relating to human extinction, i.e., our extinction, is the most gross dereliction of public duty owed by black media to black communities. But I wouldn't be surprised if it is true because such dereliction of duty is in alignment with the behavior of the black bourgeoise and/or boule for over 150 years.[112] They are sworn to serve white supremacist power elites whether democrat or republican. They have done so like watch dogs. We are all paying for their intentional negligence and for them framing misinformation to be the black popular narrative.[113] Let me explain why.

About 108 billion human beings have lived and died on earth.[114] We are 7% living human beings of that total on this planet. I think it is statistically safe to say that our species is on the downward slope of a logistic curve. In 10,000 B.C.E., there were approximately 1,000,000 to 10,000.000 homo sapiens on earth there will be about 11,000,000 billion by 2050. There was virtually no

---

[111] My point is supported by historical facts. During the 1960s the FBI paid black bookstore owners not to sale specific books written by black scholars. It was part of the Counterintelligence program initiated by J. Edger Hoover.

[112] Frazier, Franklin E; Black Bourgeoise, Free Press Paperbacks, 1962

[113] Woodrow Wilson instituted (Executive Order 2594) 'The Committee of Public Information'(1917-to 1919) to control mass media. The methods employed by the Creel Committee continue today to control black media and even black bookstores.

[114] Population Reference Bureau, 2015

meaningful human population density in relation to the land area of the planet 10,000 B.C.E. Obviously, there were far more wild animals than human beings. Those humans that were born lived very short lives. Most died within 1 year of life and most others by the age of 16 years. That is about the life span of a pet dog in human years today.

A high sex drive and the resulting reproduction rate is the only reason we survived wherever we were located. We got lucky. By 10,000 B.C.E., climate change became favorable for agriculture because global average temperatures in different regions stabilized enough to allow for the cultivation of grains like wheat, barley, oats, and maize and there was plenty of wild meat including sea food, and water. We started settled communities, domesticated some animals, refined our technologies, made up mythologies, made tooth decay normative, and thus triggered the beginning of what we call civilizations. It was a very slow process and at no time was there a guarantee of success. But I seriously wonder whether our luck has run out.

In fact, it has always been far more likely than not that our species would go extinct as had happened to all other Hominid species like ours. Life for our ancestors was no cruise on the Nile. There was only hunting and gathering or back bending hard labor from sunup to sundown. And it wasn't just the hard labor which shortened human life. There were deadly infectious bacterial and viral diseases, crocodiles, lions, and a thousand kinds of mammals, reptiles and insects that would kill and eat a human at every opportunity. I'm not trying to paint a horrid picture; it was a horrid experience for intelligent self-reflective creatures to be conscious of his or her situation and be powerless to do anything about it. Have the stage props changed? I think not. And we need to talk about that and get ready for an unimaginable scope of change on earth. It may be the last chapter in our story on earth.[115]

I'm not arguing solutions in this essay because I do not think that there are rational solutions for every problem. I do not think that we can solve the ecological problems that we have soon enough to avert human extinction. For example, as of June 6, 2021, there were 7,870,913,975 billion people on earth.[116] We are not a sequestered fraction of that number; whatever happens to the whole happens to every fraction thereof. Earth does not have the capacity for unlimited human growth.[117] And at the present rate of population growth the world population will be about 11 billion people by 2050. That adds up to more consumption of resources per person and more waste per person and machine.

For example, we now have reduced many biomes' level of sustainability.[118] In fact, in the western United States we are in a megadrought which will further erode biomes. Lake Mead is one-third below its normal water level

---

[115] Mann, Michael E; Dire Predictions: Understanding Climate Change, Penguin Random House, 2015

[116] Meadows, Donella; Limits to Growth: the 30-Year Update; Chelsea Green Publishing Company, White River Junction, Vermont, 2004

[117] Meadows, Donella; Limits to Growth: the 30-Year Update; Chelsea Green Publishing Company, White River Junction, Vermont, 2004

[118] What Drives Societal Collapse? Harvey Weiss and Raymond S. Bradley, Science 26 Jan 2001, Vol. 291, Issue 5504, pp.609-610

and Lake Powell in Utah is 45 feet below its 2020 level. And, as global average temperature increases, statistical models predict drought conditions all over the world will get worse, that means less water and dead lakes. Biomes such as forests, grasslands, lakes, wetlands, and tundra whereon thousands of species are uniquely adapted are in decline.

One collateral effect of megadroughts will be economic inflation driven by food shortages. We are right now during both economic inflation and a food shortage crisis. The basic crops which we have depended upon to sustain highly dense urban populations for the last 5,000 years are failing due to water shortages or increased droughts. Climate change has been documented as a cause of civilizational collapse before. The old Kingdom of Ta-Marry and Mediterranean Bronze age empires failed and collapsed due to climate change circa 1630 B.C.E.[119] That collapse marked the end of the Bronze age.[120] Collapse is now happening again.

The basic crops we depend upon like rise, corn, wheat, soybean, and potatoes are each sensitive to a specific range of temperatures. If, for example, drought and water shortages continue to increase in the western United States, then the California Central Valley will turn into a dessert. That is extremely important because right now 60% of all vegetables eaten in the United States come from the California Valley. The evidence in support of

---

[119] What Drives Societal Collapse? Harvey Weiss and Raymond S. Bradley, Science 26 Jan 2001, Vol. 291, Issue 5504, pp.609-610
[120] Ta Marry is the original name of Ancient Egypt. See: Black Athena, by Martin Bernal, Vol. 1

desertification in California points to bad times ahead. The Sierra mountain range bordering the California and Nevada snowpack runoff is described in 2021 as being "wiped-out.[121]

No runoff water from the snowpack will cause farmers to pump more than 60% of their water needs out of aquifers which are already estimated to be at an all-time low. Food prices will skyrocket.[122] Social instability will increase. The prospects are not good. We are on course to reach 2.2 Celsius average global temperature by 2030 or in 9 years. California is presently in a megadrought or a once in 1,200-year drought. It could last 10 to 20 or more years. Consequently, Hoover Dam and other western dams are projected to generate less electricity for Las Vegas, Los Angeles, and other western cities and towns.

Annual crop yields have been in decline worldwide. But, if present trends continue, every nation will suffer the same crop yield declines due to climate change over the course of the 21st century. The decline in crop yields along with the extinction rate of mammals and fish in

---

[121] California Department of Water Resources, California's snowpack was just 6% of normal for May 11, and 4% of the normal average for April 1, 2021.

[122] One-Third of farmland in the U.S. Has Lost Its Topsoil, Published at the Yale School of Environment, February 18, 2021

both oceans and lakes will cut human food consumption and thus human growth.[123] Watch prices go up!

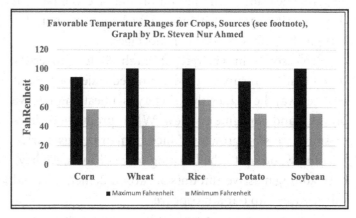

Figure 14

Global food insecurity will cut global population down from about 11 billion in 2050 to 4.5 billion by 2100 if we survive that long.[124] Our habitats are shrinking. For a short while population densities will rise as people huddle in areas they think are habitable but that in turn will only speed of the process of decline as resources there shrink even faster. The majority of African Americans are locked

---

[123] Graph Data from: Shaw (1980), Thompson (1975), Lee and Estes (1982), Willis et al. (1957), Walker (1969), Brown (1976), Ladd et al. (1902), Fabriani and Lintas (1988), Nuttonson (1965a, b), Copeland (1924), Yoshino et al. (1988), Tropical Agricultural Research Center (1987), Ymaguchi and Spurr (1964), Ng and Loomis (1984), Menzel (1983), World Potato Facts (1982)

[124] United Nations Environment Program report (2020) says "The Earth is in the midst of a Mass Extinction of life. 150-200 species of plant, insect, bird and mammals become extinct every 24 hours."

in concrete jungles. Inner cities will become literal ovens because concrete has a high thermal mass capacity, or it retains heat for a long period of time. Descendants of slaves in cities are not being taught how to prepare for extreme heat, food, and water shortages.[125]

Professor Tim Garrett of Utah State University stated that earth runs a "predetermined trajectory.[126] Put another way, he argues that society is a heat engine. We produce and consume to grow. When production slows or stops, we stop growing. Since human beings started burning wood up to the burning of fossil fuels, we have been adding massive amounts of carbon-2, methane, and sulfur gases into our atmosphere.

Each of those gases trap heat in our atmosphere like a blanket surrounding the earth. Their combined function has set in motion numerous environmental tipping points only one of which is necessary to bring us down. The trapping of heat in our atmosphere is a byproduct of our economic activities. So, the more we burn fossil fuels the higher the average global temperature will rise over hundreds of years. The greater the average global temperature rise the less habitable the earth will become for life in the oceans and on land. Garrett stated that our conserving energy "… shouldn't be any pretense that it will make a difference." Our civilizations are riding on a downward slope.

---

[125] Contemporary Climatic Analogs for 540 North American Urban areas in the late 21st century; by Matthew C. Fitzpatrick & Robert R. Dunn; Nature Communications, University of Maryland Centre for environmental Science, 2019

[126] Garrett, T. J; How persistent is civilization growth? arXiv:1101.5635v1. Published, 03/2011.

18

A Cruel and Unnatural Cycle

I disagree with the 19th century sociologist Emile Durkheim's definition that crime is "…an integral part of all healthy societies."[127] I think Durkheim was wrong. My argument is that crime, prisons, and jails are an integral part of unhealthy societies. In fact, data throughout the 20th and part of the 21st centuries demonstrate that incarceration transforms people by 'differential association' into socially disabled members and over time disables communities from which they come and to which they return.[128] Once a tipping point of population density is passed anti-cultures become self-perpetuating in communities. That in turn makes them perpetual people feeders to the criminal justice system. That is an aspect of the urban entropic effect. Those conditions can never be reversed.

Among its many offspring, prisons are the offspring of the industrial revolution. too. They are a freakish sideshow of a new world view with different assumptions

[127] Emile Durkheim; The Division of Labor in Society, 1893
[128] Edwin Sutherland, Criminology, J.B. Lippincott Co., Philadelphia,1924

on how to order society. Emile Durkheim's world view was also a product of the industrial revolution. But he never stopped to ask himself the question: why didn't prisons exist for hundreds of thousands of years of human history and then start to appear about 5000 years ago? Durkheim failed to understand that his definition of crime triggered the modern rationalization for prison systems which would operate based on a capitalist business model, i.e., a cost versus benefit ratio. What would their raw materials be? Who would benefit and who would pay the cost?

Unlike 19th century locomotives, prisons don't burn fossil fuels. Prisons transform individuals and then return them to communities socially disabled. So, prisons are a function of the exploitation of marginalized individuals and ethnic communities. They are those whose capital value for their families and community has run out. They are of no use except in the cruel and unnatural cycle of criminal act, arrest, incarceration, release and again criminal acts, arrest, re-incarceration, release.

And everyone in the system is defined by a job description which makes them Robotnik oriented. The system is a total institution and its list of rules and procedures per thousands of job descriptions attached on countless clipboards carried by robotically driven administrators and officers for over two centuries is the monotonous clickity clank of the criminal justice machine.

But illogically, along with the carceral process, there is an unwritten and subtly mixed mythological propaganda the prison disseminates to the public. It propagandizes the idea that human nature can be corrected or rehabilitated or 'made' to institutionally conform to prescribed normal behavior. But unknown to the public it does that while it simultaneously spiritually and institutionally anaesthetizes 'convicted people' so that it can cannibalize them. It destroys most people in it.

Unlike normal machines, the criminal justice system has no off switch for maintenance and repair. It has no power cord traceable to a power socket except public fear. The modern prison machine was turned on by laws, by imaginative fiat. Thus, it cannot be turned off because it is itself a function of American capitalism which necessarily digs the very human behavioral sinks prisons claim to eradicate.

Oxymoronically, the more inefficient a prison operates, the more efficient it is. Prisons and jails have never made communities safe from the stress caused by crime because prisons make behavioral sinks in communities deeper. Prisons and jails make communities unsafe because that is what makes the entire criminal justice system function. Insecurity not security is the power source which drives the criminal justice system.

Never seeing the forest for the trees, prisons destroy marriages, children, schools, whole neighborhoods. It destroys cultures and is destroying even the possibility for meaningful social action because inside prisons individuals cannot socially and meaningfully participate in growth inducing groups. They are by both state and federal law suspended in a repressive and meaningless void. So, prisons like factory smokestacks are continually contributing to ecological dysfunction when its products are released back into communities. Its pollutants are not gas, liquid, or solid. Rather, prisons sink the morale and capacity for whole populations to feel hope and to construct a vision of their future outside of prison. Prison fallout forces everyone to emotionally absorb frustration and anger. As a direct result, prison culture compounds the growth of violence in communities.[129]

Like any machine, prisons feed on energy to function. But the carceral system is monovore; it only feeds on people.[130] In Oakland California and in every urban area in America, non-white and poor people have been prison feed used to turn a macabre kind of profit return for career personnel and private businesses. An asset for the criminal justice system is determined by a calculus of depreciation per individual human life, by the subtraction of human life; that is what is counted as a success…as a credit on the prison ledger. But it is a short-term success because the confluence of millions of broken women and men over time with broken communities and extreme climate change will be yet another factor tearing America apart. The reason is simple.

Homicides and aggravated assaults are not increasing in cities like Oakland California. The tragic truth is that the rates of homicide and aggravated assaults have become as predictable as a heartbeat. Crime has ceased to be an unexpected abnormality instead crime has become normative. Therefore, we should reject 2–3-month crime data comparisons put out by the media to suggest that

---

[129] Dollard, John; Frustration and Aggression, Greenwood Press, Inc. 1939

[130] Foucault, Michel Foucault; *Discipline and Punish: the birth of Prison*. Translated by Sheridan, Alan. London: Penguin. p. 333., 1975

there is an unprecedented post pandemic crime wave. Nothing could be further from the truth. We should rather accept the long-term data that demonstrate the failure by design of the entire criminal justice system to address the collapse of communities in every city in the nation because of a deeply rooted carceral 'business as usual' orientation.[131]

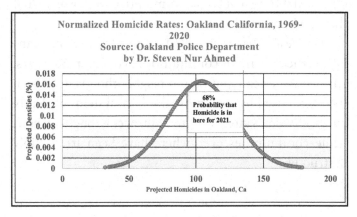

Figure 15

Every machine produces waste as a byproduct of its functioning. The truth that no one wants to hear or read or think about is that broken people cannot be made whole by prisons any more than a ball can spontaneously roll uphill. Incarceration exhausts people and makes them socially disabled for life. Socially disabled people

---

[131] "In 2008, the Pew Center on the States reported that incarceration levels had risen to a point where 1 in 100 American adults was behind bars. A second Pew study the following year added another disturbing dimension to the picture, revealing that 1 in 31 adults in the United States was either incarcerated or on probation or parole."

are buried alive in plain view for all to see. Broken people are dumped into broken communities[132]

Left therein, broken people churn out broken children to further the cruel and unnatural cycle of arrest, incarceration, release, and reincarceration. And when broken people are stacked high enough, eventually critical mass is reached. At that moment, people wake up to see for the first time that their communities are prisons. That they are in prison

Justice as it has been meted out to African Americans is injustice to their communities. For over 50 years, African American and Latino neighborhoods have been the places used by the criminal justice system to silently bury individuals alive. The consequences wrought on non-white communities everywhere have been irreversibly destructive.

---

[132] Gottschalk, Marie; The Prison and the Gallows: the Politics of Mass Incarceration in America; Cambridge University Press, 2006

19

Murder On the Yard

A tourist standing in the Oakland hills and having a panoramic view of the city from above without having had a micro-view from within its hollowed streets could never imagine the things that go down at sunset and in the wee hours of the morning. They would not see what we who live therein see day and night. Something has happened to all of us. I think what has happened is irreversible. We are victims of the urban entropic effect.

African American neighborhoods have been expeditiously destroyed by prisons and jails nationwide over the past fifty-one years. The problem is not social change per se because change can give rise to useful values. Furthermore, social structures always change from within just as DNA within genes and genes within cells carry codes for anatomical changes in our bodies. But sometimes errors or mutations occur in DNA which when passed on from one generation to the next causes permanent anatomical changes in a whole species.

Likewise, neighborhoods or communities normally change slowly from within because beliefs are coded into traditional behaviors which in turn are imitated by children by instruction thereby perpetuating the culture. The jail or prison incarceration process is instruction by imitation too, but it is an error or variance in the life orientation of people who are incarcerated.

Over time, when millions of individuals are institutionally processed through prisons and jails, their traditional beliefs or codes are broken. If we only focus on individuals who are incarcerated, we miss the millions who are simultaneously incarcerated. The incarceration of millions of African Americans thus represents cultural variance in the coded beliefs and collective social practices of whole populations. New instructions, the errors, are then passed on orally and behaviorally from one generation after another until the ratio of tradition to prison anti-culture becomes biased in favor of anti-culture. Some social scientists will use the generalized phrase social change to describe the process but in truth it is a process of the social disorder of ethnic institutions.[133]

The signs of cultural decay in our communities are self-evident. For example, a friend of mine named Chauncy Bailey was shot in the face by a shotgun blast on 14th street downtown Oakland in broad daylight August 2007; on March 21, 2009, four Oakland police officers were murdered and one wounded in broad daylight in east Oakland; a father was beaten to death in front of his son in broad daylight in April of 2010; a three year old child was gunned down in August 2011; more children were continued to be shot in 2012 and the number of

---

[133] Irving Goffman, Asylums: Essays on the Social Situation of Mental Patients and Other Inmates, Anchor Press, 1961

shootings and homicides continued to rise in the city of Oakland that year for a grand total of one hundred thirty-one for the year 2012. As of December 2021, the murder rate constituted a 42% increase over the 2010 murder rate and is consistent with an average of one hundred-nine murders over the fifty-one years.

In Oakland, most homicide victims and perpetrators have been descendants of slavery with an increasing number of Latinos as population ethnic mixtures in the city change. Many citizens black and white wonder 'what is going on' because they don't see the institutional connections. The answer to that question is complex not simple. And the solutions for it are as complex as the problems are. But the backdrop to much of the tragedies occurring in African American neighborhoods is telling.

There has been a slow but consistent cultural transplantation of culture from prisons and jails into every major urban center in the United States.

The breakdown is the crack cocaine epidemic of the 1970s through 1990s which accounts for a general breakdown in African American neighborhoods. It is because of prison yard counterculture manufactured in prisons and jails and taken into cities like Oakland, Ca. Generation by generation, the process of culture transplantation has broken to pieces and swept aside an older traditional African American way of life. The old coded beliefs have been eroded by new codes of belief and practice. Traditional civil behaviors are nearly completely displaced now.

African American culture today is not the same culture which emerged from the post-civil war freedmen culture. That traditional culture was driven by freed men and women and had a strong orientation for self-sufficiency and expansion of civil rights and inclusion in the United States. On the other hand, a culture of parolees who are best described as a 'behavioral sink' are never set free from their stigma and punishment.[134] They are not allowed to ever have hopes rekindled for a self-determined future. Their culture is a prison-yard culture fashioned for them within the confines of total institutions.[135] Parolees live devitalized and dependent lives because they are prescribed the role 'feeder' of the prison industrial complex for life. The whole criminal justice system depends upon them to stay in character and to stick to the script given to them in urban concentration centers. It did not have to be that way.

For decades, the California Department of Corrections and Rehabilitation has ignored an important parole option which could have reduced the concentration of marginalized parolees in cities with high crime rates like Oakland. The California Penal Code states specifically in Section 3000, Article 1, subsection 30039(a) that a parolee "…shall be returned to the county that was the last legal residence of the inmate prior to his or her incarceration."[136] Many people presume it to be an exclusive parole policy. However, there is also another

---

[134] John B. Calhoun, A Behavioral Sink, in E.L. Bliss (ed.) Roots of Behavior, New York: Harper, 1962b

[135] Goffman, Erving, Essays on the Social Situation of Mental Patients and other Inmates, by Erving Goffman; Anchor Books, 1961

[136] California Penal Code, Unabridged Criminal Justice Edition, 2017

less publicly known option. It is subsection 30039(b) which states in part: "...an inmate may be returned to another county if that would be in the best interests of the public." Subsection 30039(b) is rarely used and is at the heart of the rise of chaos in predominately black communities over the last 50 years.

I think it has been an intentional racist policy to destroy individuals' integrity and the basic institutions which we depend upon, i.e., families, schools, family, and marketplace opportunities. In short, a long-term policy of ethnic cleansing has been and is being perpetrated in cities like Oakland against black people. Statistical analysis below supports my claim.[137] It also paved the way for regentrification. The regentrification of Oakland and the decline of the black population is correlated with a rise in incarceration and deepening dysfunction in black communities. Incarceration and the parole policy of the California Department of Correction and Rehabilitation is the cause of the growth of anti-culture in black communities. The exponential decline and damage is irreversible.

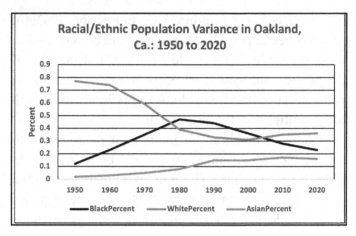

Figure 16

Prison yard values are culturally transmitted onto black communities nationwide. Those values have had far reaching collateral effects on many individuals in many communities because of an increasing national and state incarceration rate over the past fifty-one years. There are many examples. For instance, Oakland, California is city where for more than fifty-one years generation after generation of parolees and probationers have slowly increased in percentage in comparison to non-parolees and probationers. They are compelled to live impoverished lives concentrated in small pockets of cities without full enjoyment of the bill of rights.

My thesis is predicated on the fact that the county probation and state parolee populations in Alameda County are respectively approximately 8,969 probationers in 2020 and 4,345 parolees in of 2010.[138] What we are dealing with is the high likelihood that about twenty percent of

---

[138] Urban Strategies Council, 2010

Oakland's population has been or is incarcerated or has been or is in jail over the past fifty-one years. In some areas of the city that percent is even higher. The parolee population density relative to the non-parolee population density has been growing for fifty years. No wonder that violent crimes occur in a narrow section of Oakland between the 880 and 580 freeways.[139] The California Department of Corrections and Rehabilitation compel parolees to live in that narrow strip after release from prison. Paroling so many people there is like throwing a lighted match into a barrel of gasoline. We are faced with horrific long-term consequences. We are faced with the negative transformation of culture.

Over thirty percent of Oakland's population have suffered a murdered relative, friend, or associate. Such deep and pervasive sorrow felt by citizens sours the very core of interpersonal relations. It seeps down into the hearts of children and traumatizes them for life. Consequently, Oakland is a city made up of thousands of depressed individuals because they are traumatized by an anti-culture of violence. A pall hangs over the whole city, not just impoverished neighborhoods, as would a thick smog shroud the many processions of those people carrying their dead through its streets every 3.5 days to a cemetery. There is no sign which can be pointed to that says the blood lust will wane within a reasonable time

---

[139] Source: CA Department of Corrections and Rehabilitation; US Census; Bradford Map Co. Inc., Urban Strategies Council, Date Saved 10/13/2010

because blood lusting has become a way of life.[140] It's part of the total institutional script for men and women living on the fringes of society.

All institutions are feeling the stress of the prison yard culture. Poor families cannot carry the burden it puts upon them. Even Congress has been tinkering with a 'Second Chance Act' because the widespread discrimination of ex-felons is shoring up the prison yard anti-culture and causing it to burst all social levees such as prisons, jails, parole, and probation departments. AB 109 signed into law on April 5th, 2011, will increase the rate of cultural disintegration in Oakland because the county jail 'levees will not hold because over 65% of the persons incarcerated and staying in character return to society, eventually.

It is causing a facial change in communities, too, as more militarized armed guards block the sunlight in what had been historically recognized safe zones like hospital, supermarkets, college campuses, restaurants, and funeral gatherings. People there are feeling the oxymoronic nature of their 'guarded liberty'. They are beginning to feel the crunch caused by police occupation of the 'land of the free'. They are beginning to apply the concept of ecological phrase 'dead zone' to their neighborhoods. They too feel incarcerated.

Moreover, such environments incubate the prison yard anti-culture mind-set because it is anti-culture which submerges their constitutional freedoms to the demands of police necessity. It has turned police officers into

---

[140] When and Where Does Crime Occur in Oakland, Law.bereley. edu, (January 2008 – July 2013), The Chief Justice Earl Warren Institute on Law and Social Policy

jailers; it has turned their oath of service and protection to community into a visceral obsessive compulsion to control everyone. Their fear of wrongdoers is now greater than the fear wrongdoers have of them. We should not be surprised, therefore, that such disaffection is the guard-convict syndrome. It too has become a characteristic of the neighborhood. It is now a permanent characteristic of those who live in neighborhoods throughout the nation.

The police, surrounded by a community of mistrusted parolees and probationers, cease to trust the public because the public is increasingly on parole, off parole, or predominantly are the children of parolees who were initiated into the prison yard culture on visitation days. So, they cease to serve the public because they do not recognize it as a free community of citizens. To them, that community has become indistinguishable from the mass of marginalized parolees.

The police community is an island unto itself as much a fringe group as the parolees and equally mistrusted and dangerous to the public. On August 13, 2011, a homeless man raised a stick in the presence of an Oakland police officer. That man was shot dead. It's happening everywhere; sometimes phrased as 'stand your ground' or 'He was wearing a hoodie'; 'He was sagging; 'I feared for my life' or 'I thought he was reaching for a gun.' Each are but rationalizations for murder. To convert murder to justifiable homicide disproportionally applied to African American males who are presumed guilty at birth and to be feed for the prison industrial complex or premature death.

The prison yard culture is a product of the prison

industrial complex; it runs an ever-rolling assembly line. Its only product is designed to be uselessness. It is the antithesis of the infinitive 'to be'. It thrives because it feeds on the anxieties of repressed populations of men and women outside prisons. Its frenzy to feed never wanes because it's appetite, its hunger, is without limit; it is a demonically voracious system. It is just as dehumanizing as the military industrial complex. It is a boa constrictor that grips people of all ages and intwines itself around them squeezing them until whatever they were to their mothers in their innocence is dies and goes unremembered. Like a Boa, prisons profit off the human flesh, misery, and ignorance of those who live on its hunting grounds.

Traditional icons for civil rights no longer pepper public consciousness and inspire hope like Dr. Martin Luther King and Malcom X. Communities can no longer effectively regenerate useful life values through their offspring because institutions therein have been crippled. Now, many of their parents reflexively live the prison-yard anti-culture A shift in the axis of life interests has elevated the prison yard anti-culture and has made it more effective in transmitting its values to at least three generations of descendants of slaves.[141]

Its logic is now normative. Its own icons are empty caricatures manufactured by the prison yard culture and its entertainment spin offs which glorify its debauchery. Its anti-cultural purpose illogical but nevertheless is the purpose for which it was designed. It is to trigger visceral impulses in children that are inversely proportionate to intellectual and spiritual focus and growth. It has its own

---

[141] Generations X, Millennials, and Gen. Z

rites of passage for its children, its own ceremonial baptism in its static atmospheres...on visiting day. Children, learn the strip search and get ready for the arrest hunt.

White supremacist intellectuals in government, especially the demographic statisticians, could foresee through their statistical population models the prospect of our current predicament over fifty years ago. They could see the rise of chaos in black communities in the data, the raw numbers, as clearly as we see far away galaxies through the lens of the Hubble space telescope. Despite that they committed criminal negligence and in so doing committed a crime against humanity, yet again, on descendants of slaves.

20

Permutations

Today, I was thinking about a geological process called 'tectonic plate drift'. For billions of years, the continents we live on have been drifting, floating on top of the earth's mantle, or subducting beneath the earth's crust and mantle. The mantle has plasticity and is a molten rock part of the earth's interior. It is churned by the force of gravity ad it heats up and cools down molten rock.

The result of this repetitive temperature variation is that the surface of the earth undergoes continuous change of its geographical positions and thus makes different continental formations. Sometimes they are combined and sometimes divided and sometimes they are subducted and lost forever in our earth's molten core.

This constant flux and instability then turned my thoughts to the very complex and dysfunctional social, environmental, and political situation we live in. On all levels, the United States is in crises mode as is the whole world. It's not quite what crises have typically been in the past.

On the social horizon, there are no sound logical solutions to the countless problems we face. That is so because the dramatic stage whereon we act out our lives was founded upon what we know to be false ideas or assumptions. For example, the idea that some people are born to be slaves or that society is a mirror image of predator and prey relations in the wilds. That kind of illogical thinking inevitably makes more links in a long chain of destructive decisions and actions which warp the fabric of our social relations.

The philosopher Plato understood the inevitable end of illogical thinking. He made it clear in his 'allegory of the cave' that those people who draw conclusions from false premises or 'shadows on the wall' and then act on those conclusions are doomed to spiritual emptiness and ultimate social collapse.[142]

I understand both scientifically and spiritually what is driving the mass dysfunction which makes America a sick society. I know that most human beings are driven unconsciously by their instincts namely anxiety and sexuality. But in combination with those basic instincts there generally exists far weaker logical thinking in relation to our instincts exercised most of the time by most of the people. That is precisely why social relations at all levels are more likely to go awry.

For example, why would a person who is obese and at risk for dozens of diseases and a premature death continue to consume a diet that will ultimately kill him or her? Why would they allow their children to do so? Knowing full well that what confronts them are but two alternatives: change or die.

I understand that some very intelligent people

---

[142] Plato's Republic

understand those unconscious biological drives. They have worked hard to master methods of manipulating the collective unconscious for the sole purposes of economically exploiting the environment, control of mass populations of people and other animals, and ruling over them. Despite the intelligence of the power elite, they intentionally do wrong to others for monetary profit and or simply for pleasure.

Some intelligent people who are determined to benefit themselves at the expense of others believe in and practice scientific racism or social Darwinism. Social Darwinism is predicated on the fallacious premise that there is an absolute natural standard of fitness by means of which unfit human beings can be identified. From that premise, it is deduced that once the unfit are identified they can be eliminated effectively washing the gene pool clean and fit.

A glaring antithesis to their claim that there is an absolute standard of natural human fitness is their claim that evolutionary change is a law of organic nature. Their argument for evolutionary change is antithetical to their idea of an absolute standard of fitness because evolutionary change presupposes genetic and phenotypical maladjustment to a broader natural environment. In short, evolutionary change means that a specie is in a constant a state of unfitness, and thus on the chopping block, and subject for natural elimination.

This may seem a stretch, but for example, a pattern of lowered human I.Q. in a population could be a signal of human brain adaption in reverse. A cerebral reversal in humans to restore balance between the human species and nature at large. Such a restoration of balance in the natural environment would save both humans and nature from technological destruction.

Put another way, if we toxify the environment, in the same proportion the environment toxifies our bodies. If we make nature at large infertile, then proportionately nature makes us infertile at large. We are at a disadvantage in that kind of action and reaction contest with nature because nature is bigger than us and because nature has masterfully eliminated trillions of species before us and yet continues to move along its course with or without carrying life on its back. I do not suggest that nature is personal; nature is very impersonal in its relation to us. It's just the way it rolls independently of us and life in general.

Though such mythological beliefs have been expressed by people dating back far into ancient human history long before Charles Darwin wrote his book which gave rise to the phrase: "Survival of the Fit." Power elites down through the ages have practiced the survival of the fit ideology on the premise that human reason or rationality are necessarily to be driven by human unconscious instincts. The general acceptance of social Darwinism by most people today has made a wide pathway for the worst kind of people to ascend to the top of our social hierarchies where decisions affecting billions of people are made. The result is now a disaster.

For example, it has become an established fact that human industries have released billions of tons of carbon dioxide, and methane into the atmosphere for over the last one hundred years. Those gases in the atmosphere are correlated with a 1-degree Celsius rise in global warming and extreme weather climate change over the last 100 years.

Industries which polluted the atmosphere were allowed to operate even though it was reported by the Journal of Science in 1896 that the release of those gases caused by burning fossil fuels would cause a greenhouse effect thus making the earth surface temperature warmer. Why?

If we assume that intelligent people who owned those industries and politicians who legally sanctioned toxic industries knew how to do a basic scientific cost/benefit analysis or a risk analysis of the long-term consequences of 'the greenhouse effect' on the global environment, that begs the question: why did they persist in doing what they knew would eventually cause a global crisis and death to billions of people in the future?

That answer is simple. Those intelligent psychopaths didn't give a flying ducks quack about the future of billions of people nor the planet earth hundreds of years into the future after they are dead. They viewed only short-term benefits and costs to them during their lifetime.

They rationally concluded that what happens to the planet and the animals on it after they are dead is irrelevant to what they wanted in their lifetime. They are attracted to money, fame, power, control, status, prestige, and all other possible pleasures in their lifetime or in the here and now. They figured that once they were dead that nothing on earth or for that matter in the universe could either benefit or cost them nor put them at risk of harm because they believed that at death they simply cease to exist. They were selfish. It's that simple.

All intelligent psychopathic power elite, oligarchs, or tyrants operate on that same premise because they have no conscience, nor the compassion or empathetic feelings. Therefore, most people suffer politically from what is known as a kakistocracy. Kakistocracy means a government controlled by the least qualified or most unprincipled citizens. Eventually, such people destroy themselves and are now working on the destruction of the world we have come to know is our only home.

I understand that the kind of economic exploitation we suffer is not unique to our society. It overlaps all societies and exists at every class or caste level, within every ethnicity or race and everywhere in the world it has existed throughout history. That simply underscores the fact that we have yet to find a way to vet psychopaths out of our economic and political systems or to prevent them from infiltrating our political systems.

I understand the connection between humans' biological instincts and social/economic slavery. Intelligent people who are also psychopathic know that they can enslave most people to do their will by addicting them to substances of all kinds ranging from food to drugs, material possessions and status, or false beliefs. Or they can enslave most people by instilling in them fear of pain and or death.

Yet, all people are at least minimally rational unless they are intellectually defective. And most people can understand when they are being short changed and by whom as one would feel when he or she is cheated in a supermarket because they do not receive the correct change in exchange for a purchase.

But most people tacitly accept servitude to a power elite rather than choose to be free. In other words, they internalize subconsciously a self-image of being a slave and then through that internalized image interpret their social relations as inferior to the political and economic power elite. They then go about acting out accordingly. This is true everywhere even though cultures differ throughout the world.

I started this talk with some thoughts I had on continental drift. For me it indicates that no matter how powerful or large a thing may appear to be whether it be empires, nations, clans, tribes, and individuals, each one of them will come to its end and be changed within the context of an ever-changing combination of matter. This is not a little-known law of nature.

21

False Hope is Hopelessness

I believe that the study history is a science. Science is driven to inferences by empirical evidence. Historians who employ the empirical method proceed in the field to gather forensic and authentic documentary facts as would an investigator at the scene of a crime. Those who don't are not historians. If there are not supportive facts about the past, then history is inconclusive. Mythologists are not historians. Hearsay and presuppositions about the past are not admissible as a true representation of the past.

At this crucial point in our sojourn in America, those who consider history must decide whether they will be empirical. Descendants of slavery are sensitive to this issue because it is mythology which was used to rationalize our slavery. I say our slavery because we who are alive are the organic extension through space and time of every slave that ever lived during legalized slavery in the United States. We are literally them.

I read a book entitled: 'The Devil You Know'. The book was written by Charles M. Blow. He put forth a very weak argument for a reversed migration of black people to southern states. Blow advocated what he called a simple proposition. He states in his book: "The proposition is simple as many black descendants of the Great Migration as possible should return to the South from which their ancestors fled. They should do so with moral and political intentionality. And as many Black people not descendants of American slavery as possible should join in their resettlement."[143] This is one of the most ill-conceived proposals to African Americans this century. Migration northward was for the opposite economic conditions than what conditions exist in the southern states today. The southern states are the poorest states in the nation and thus do not have the infrastructure to absorb black descendants of the great migration.

The present population of all African Americans in the United States is approximately 46,000,000 (million) persons, but only if you count all people from Africa. We can't do that. We can't count all people of African descendent because they are different ethnicities or cultures as descendants of slavery are a different ethnic group. Furthermore, we can't because our population characteristics are changing rapidly and not for the better in comparison to theirs. Let's dissect our population starting with baby boomer descendants of slaves. The data is a few years old, but it makes the point clearly,

The baby boom generation officially started in 1945. It officially ended in 1964. Their age range is 57 to 75 years, today. That constitutes about 71.6 million people. Now, of that number, approximately 7 million are descendants of slaves. So, they too constitute an age range of 57 to 75 years

---

[143] Charles M. Blow, The Devil You Know: A Black Power Manifesto, HarperCollins Publishers, 2021 p.31

of age, today. In the long run, by the year 2064, nearly all baby boomer descendants of slave will be dead. Black baby boomers are retiring at a rate of about 700 persons per day. When we hold those figures in mind and combine them with another rapidly changing characteristic of the descendent of slavery population, the magnitude of our population problem should dawn on you. First, let's turn now to our population reproduction rate.

The birth rate of descendants of slaves has been declining for at least 10 years. Our population decline is most evidenced by a negative growth rate of the Age Specific Fertility Rate (ASFR).[144] For example, the fertility rate of descendants of slaves has dropped to 1.7 babies for all women between the ages of 15 and 45 years. What that means is that the population of descendants of slaves is not even breaking even at 2.1 babies born to all women descendants of slaves over a 1-year period. The year 2021 will be a birth and death rate disaster for us because of the covid-19 disaster.

If we continue at this rate over the next 9 years our population will reduce by approximately 3,098,781. Even more so, if we subtract the approximately 5,000,000 African Immigrants and their children then the number of descendants of slaves will be even more startling at 33,098,781 African Americans by 2030. We are not growing anymore.

---

[144] At present the population rate of change is -0.23 per 9 to 10 years as depicted on graph 3 above.

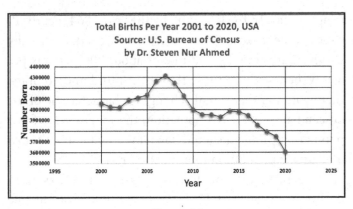

Figure 16

If we assume that at least half of all baby boomer descendants of slave will be dead by 2030, then shave another 3,500,000 million people off our population projection leaving us with approximately 29, 598,781 persons. That is a far cry from the 70 million people projected by Dr. James Taylor. And at the same time our population is undergoing such significant changes, the African immigrant population is projected to grow.

Charles Blow explicitly claimed that descendants of slaves can take over the political institutions by the sheer weight of our voting power once the migration is set in motion and we settle there. He failed to stoke his memory of larger urban populations like Atlanta, Baltimore, Harlem, Oakland, Compton, and other cities in which black folks tried and failed to 'take over' the political apparatuses. We couldn't 'take over' those cities because black folk did not have nor do they have now adequate capital to do so. Neither did they have control over some of the local economic infrastructures and their justice systems in a single city or town in the United States.

The fate of black people who were elected to mayoral offices by great voter turnouts of black people and the appointment of bureaucrats was quickly exposed for what it was. Their predetermined political path was to serve the interests of local white capital and political interest groups. Their role was simply that of figurehead. That is all that would result in Mississippi now even with Chokwe Lumumba as mayor of the city of Jackson, the state capital of Mississippi.

I know that pattern all too well having lived in Oakland California and seen three impotent black mayors oversee the exodus of capital infrastructure, the attendant loss of thousands of jobs, and the ongoing humiliation of a whole community by white supremacist police officers during their tenures.[145] Absolutely nothing got better in Oakland. In fact, their tenures coincided with the beginning of the crack cocaine epidemic thru its zenith and the huge incarceration rate of black people, breakdown of thousands of family structures, and increasing dysfunction of a once stable public school system.

Mississippi is ranked 50th (the worst) on the list of the poorest states in the nation. Mississippi has a poverty rate of 19.6 percent; descendants of slavery have a poverty rate of 30.8%. More people migrate out of that state than migrate into it. By every major social and economic indicator, generally, the conditions African Americans suffer in Mississippi are hopeless. In the waning days of the United States empire and onset of climate change, the situation will get worse. Louisiana, Arkansas, South

---

[145] Lionel Wilson (1977 to 1991, Elihu Harris (1991 to 1999, and Ronald Dellums (2007 to 2011)

Carolina, Florida, and Tennessee are all similar. Anyone who paints a phantasy of reverse migration in your mind as a solution for the ills of descendants of slaves' political and economic problems is either grossly misinformed or selling you false hope in what is a hopeless situation.

And would they tell us where all the millions of poor black folks in the north, northeast, and west will gather the means to 'reverse migrate' to the so- called 'ancestral' homeland? And even if they did, by what means would they live their lives? What schools would their children attend? But the data makes these questions moot because marriage in the black community is on decline. What families? Single parent households? There is a negative correlation between the marriage rate and the abortion rate in the black population. The marriage rate goes down to 23% in 2021 and is projected to decline even further to approximately 14% while over the same span of years the black abortion rate held at 32% (17,600,000 fetuses) of all abortions. Whether you are pro or con abortion, you must admit populations don't recover that amount of population decline.

It reminds me of the Soviet Union's population loss during world War II at 27,000,000 people. They have never demographically recovered from that population loss. We won't recover from ours either.

I think there are no satisfactory answers to any of these questions. If there were answers to those questions they would have been answered long, long ago by more earnest individuals than Blow and Taylor.

22

The U.S. is Economy Not Democracy

Right wing political and religious conservatives in the United States criticize the theory of evolution which assumes that evolutionary change is inevitable. Running parallel to their intolerance to the science of Zoology, they promote political policies or laws to artificially prevent changes to their economic marketplaces. Their efforts have the effect of reinforcing the mythological world view that an unchanging socio/economic hierarchy was pre-determined by an 'invisible' hand and that they are its guardians.

Their marketplaces can appear complex on the surface especially when mathematized in their high-level university course books. But upon scrutiny there are only a few gears at the base of the marketplaces which turn the whole system to make it function. Its energy combustion sources are human labor and the consumption of goods and services capacities. That is what drives all the gears which generate wealth at every stratum of society. Basic texts on non-white ethnic communities are inescapably revealing on how the system really works.

Since before the inception of the United States,

Africans, Mexicans, Asians, and Native Americans have been turning the marketplace gears for centuries. The use of their labor energy enabled the amassment of economic wealth in gold, silver, and land by white elites across many generations. Africans were enslaved and Mexicans were victims of larceny in violation of the Fifth Amendment of the U.S. Constitution after the Mexican American war. Their labor energy was subsequently exploited as farm laborers under the Bracero program in 1942 in California. Asians' land and property was taken on many occasions in the 19th and 20th centuries. Chinese were denied citizenship until 1952. And larceny was legalized against the Indigenous tribes throughout north America. Most of us know very few details about the exploitation against those ethnic groups.

I face the undeniable fact about the history of the United States. All non-white people were initially allowed into the United States to either be slaves or provide cheap labor energy to drive the gears of a prevailing economy whether it was agricultural or industrial.

Let's face an undeniable fact about American capitalism. It is not natural law; it is an applied theory. A rational theory differs radically from a 'law of nature. A rational theory is imperfectly applied to every changing circumstance whereas a natural law is consistently constant. For example, gravity works the same way everywhere on earth independently of our social conditions, whereas capitalism being a social construction varies in its application from place to place. The theory of capitalism is attributed to Adam Smith who was not a scientist. He was an ethical and economic philosopher.

If you have some college education, then you probably know that your first course on economics taught you some fundamental assumptions about the marketplace. One assumption is that there is an open market. However, we know that the market is not open. Either governmental controls guide the market or oligarchs or gangsters. We were taught that demand determines supply, but that is not true. A monopoly interest in a product can determine demand if it prevents other competitors from selling in a market or under producing a product. There are other examples, too.

You were taught that the value assigned to goods and services is driven by the demand of consumers. That the price of goods and services vary as demand for them vary. That is false. When monopoly interests control production of goods, they can set prices independently of consumer demand by artificially limiting or increasing production of goods or services. In college, economics is taught like physics. The mystique of capitalism is created by a façade of differential and integral calculus formulae use to analyze ideal market conditions which never exist. Your best examples are the great depression and the economic recession of 2008. Both were caused by market manipulation or financial fraud.

So, if capitalism is an art not a science, then it can be done away with and replaced by another kind of economic model. It is a system which can be adjusted depending upon human needs as circumstances change. That means that our economic priorities can rearranged. For example, 14,600,000 U.S. citizens lost their health care during covid-19 between 2020 and 2021 compared to zero in every

European nation[146] And, our government spent over $6.4 trillion dollars over 20 years on wars in the Middle East and Central Asia.[147] That money was spent rather than forgive student debt now hovering at $1,710,000,000.00 dollars (trillion)! And, no, reparations to descendants of slaves are not even on a list of things to do.

I believe that reasonable people would agree on what is more important. If such a person were asked 'do we collectively and individually have greater value than the military industrial complex?' that person would answer, yes. Then why isn't the economic system in the United States directed at the betterment of its citizens? I think is because American citizens are not in control of the government which claims to be a democracy. America is an economy not a democracy. America is ruled by oligarchs not governed by 'the marketplace'.

American history suggests that in each generation some people are recruited and socialized to think illogically about the value of life on earth. They arrive at the erroneous conclusion that they are inherently better than other people and that the earth is just for their pleasure based upon concocted standards. For instance, we know that during era of slavery, genocide of indigenous peoples, Jim Crow, and share cropping the exploitation of some peoples' labor energy was rationalized based on

---

[146] Public Citizen@Public_Citizen Working people who lost health care during the pandemic.

[147] America has spent $6.4 trillion on wars in the Middle East and Asia since 2001, a new study says, by Amanda Macias, November 20, 2019, The report, from Watson Institute of International and Public Affairs at Brown University,

mythologies or pseudo-science propagandized to both literate and illiterate white people as truth or natural law. There are institutionalized narratives which propel that kind of socialization.

There are prevailing myths that life in the United States would be miserable without the American form of capitalism. Such myths are the product of propaganda just as is the myth that America is a functional democracy. If justice has to do with how, when, where, how much, and to whom we distribute benefits to people in society, then by our sentimental attachments and actions in the marketplace we are not encouraging unbiased justice in our marketplaces.[148]

Think about your family at the dinner table. Sentimental attachment to family members stokes in each member feelings of fairness when putting food on each other's plate. How is it that we lose that feeling of justice outside our homes? It is obvious to most people that feelings of fairness for others diminish outside the home. The power of the 'invisible hand' of oligarchs, deceased and living, have predetermined that there always be a constant of disproportionality at work in the allocation of resources and that disproportionality be excused as a necessary byproduct of prosperity in the United States. At least 33% of the population have barely enough to subsist on or are of the over 500,000 homeless people in the United States who have nothing no housing shelter. A disproportionate number of the homeless are descendants of slaves who were never

---

[148] Lasswell H; Politics: Who Gets What, When How? Lasswell H., New York McGraw-Hill, 1936

economically vested in the United States. While 40% of all wealth in the United States is inherited by 1% of the population many of whom are descendants of slave masters or shareholders in corporations which trafficked African slaves.[149]

---

[149] Kessler, Denis, and Andre Masson (1989); "Bequests and Wealth Accumulation: Are Some Pieces of the Puzzle Missing," Journal of Economic Perspectives, Vol. 3, No.3, pp.141-152.

23

The Pentagon UFO Report

Congress mandated, in the "committee comment" section of the Intelligence Authorization Act for Fiscal Year 2021 as printed on June 17, 2020, that the Pentagon must release all information it has on UFOs. I think that after the disclosure we will undergo mass altered consciousness. It will be greater than that of any other event in human history. The way we perceive reality will change seemingly overnight on a scale equal to the Toba super volcanic explosion 70,000 years ago.

I don't mean that time will stop. Nor do I mean that buildings will collapse. People will get up to do their 'thing' everywhere in whatever way they eke out a living. So generally, social structures will appear to remain stable. But beneath the surface of our perception something deep down in all of us and in our collective subconscious will be upheaved.

Old paradigms and the assumptions that support them will collapse and with their collapse will be gone the ancient ways we have perceived our relations to others, ecosystems, and our place on Earth. Slowly, but surely, all of us will come to know that we human beings are not special and probably not unique either except in the mind of God. And further, that here we are at the bottom of a much more complex and materially unalterable intelligence hierarchy stretching across the vastness of the Milky Way than we could have ever possibly have imagined.

That collapse will be inevitable after the UFO Pentagon disclosure. First, most people tend to have a conditioned need for a nod from government before they accept facts from non-governmental sources. That is not as true today as it was in the 1950s, but there are still enough people with that kind of mentality to churn up controversy where there should be none. Secondly, collapse will occur because our social relations are built and sustained by subconscious virtual stereotypes and sentimental bonds. What we do physically are but reactions to mutually shared meanings in our constructed virtual social realities. The best example is the language we share. Our languages are symbolic and exist only in our minds.

Paradigm collapse will result with the dissipation of our subconsciously shared meanings which is analogous to a couple falling out of love with one another or other groups of persons. A collapse of material associations will follow necessarily at different rates of speed.

What you see below is a picture I took 11 years ago. It is a picture of an unidentified aerial phenomenon hovering over the Lawrence Livermore Lab in Pleasanton California. I is hard evidence that UFOs exists. They have been and are seen all over the world.

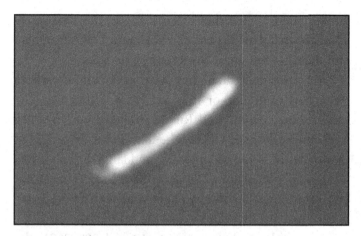

Photo 2 photo by Steven Nur Ahmed

I'm sure by now all of you are aware of the leaked information concerning Naval pilots observing flying objects over the ocean in California, dated 2004. Naval battle ships also reported a fleet of UFOs pacing them as they moved through the ocean 125 miles off the coast of San Diego, California dated 2019. Their observations are not the only time UFOs have been observed by pilots. UFOs have been doing whatever they want to do when they want to do it and going wherever they choose to go on earth for as long as records go back.

After the publication of a UFO article, dated December 16, 2017, revealing expenditures on UFO investigation along with leaked videos taken by navy fighter pilots the Pentagon confirmed the pictures and videos taken by fighter jet pilots as real or authentic.[150] The Pentagon also said that the UFOs were not technologies produced by the

---

[150] *Glowing Auras and 'Black Money'; The Pentagon's Mysterious U.F.O. Program,* New York Times, December 16, 2017

United States; when they admitted that, they indirectly admitted that they do not know where the UFOs originate and that they are not U.S. secret technologies.

My position is that they have never known where the UFOs originate, or they are lying. Either way our government, China, and Russia singularly or in unity have no power over UFOs. The aliens that drive UFOs, dominate the skies, oceans, seas, and lakes on Earth. We are not apex predators. We never have been. That is not just a game changer, that is a new game with a new player at the table. And we don't know the rules of the game.

So, sometime between June 1st and 30th, 2021, the Pentagon is going to release their report containing what it knows about UFOs. The report should date back decades going back to the 1940s. The lies used in the past to fool or misinform the public will no longer work do in large part to cell phone cameras possessed by the public at large and smarter youthful generations. No, they are not weather balloons; no, they are not swamp gas burps; no, they are not meteorites; no, fighter jet pilots carrying nuclear tipped missiles were not hallucinating.

I do not expect the Pentagon to release all the information that they possess. One of the strategies used for decades has been to control the access to UFO information through disinformation. Governmental agencies have long mastered methods of psyops to misinform the American people through third parties.[151] Since World War II they have deliberately misinformed the public about the existence of other forms of intelligent life that obviously have higher intelligence and technology than anything possessed today by human beings.

A collateral effect of the Pentagon report will highlight the control it has welded over news media, scientists, and religious agents because through them evidence has been suppressed or information distorted causing sober public discussion on the reality of UFOs to be stigmatized for decades. They have successfully controlled collective awareness about UFOs just as the Catholic Church inserted passages into the New Testament and suppressed learning of mathematics and science to control collective awareness during the medieval ages. Of course, during slavery Africans were prohibited from learning to read and write. So great was the need to suppressed consciousness of slaves that on the day of self-taught mathematician Benjamin Banneker's funeral in 1806 all the books he wrote on mathematics were burned by a mob of white supremacists.

But I do think that what the Pentagon does release will change forever how we perceive our place on Earth and in the small fragment of the solar system and universe that we are now studying.

Very important questions about UFOs and their

---

[151] "Psychological operations (PSYOPS) are operations to convey selected information and indicators to audiences to influence their emotions, motives, and objective reasoning, and ultimately the behavior of governments, organizations, groups, and individuals." Wikipedia

drivers naturally arise. Are the UFOs doing psych opts on humanity? Are they extraterrestrial? Do they do interstellar travel? If so, how do they cover such vast distances measuring light years or trillions of miles? Or are they a species of life that originated on this planet long before us and now occupy the oceans parallel to our cultures? Are there 1, 2, 3 or more alien species here? Is their DNA Hominid? Are they mammals? What do they eat? Do they eat meat? Is our atmosphere inhospitable to them? Has there been face to face contact made by government officials with some of the aliens? Do they have working agreements with governments? Are they controlling other governments through the agency of the U.S. government? Do they provoke warfare between human governments?

There are many unanswered questions. But this I do know. We are in the fog of a paradigm shift on many different social levels. Hundreds if not thousands of Bronze Age world views that we have used to interpret our experiences and place on earth will being shattered. There is great destabilizing cognitive dissonance in the population. Our histories will need to be rewritten. Our primate origin on earth will be clarified. Governments and religions will fall. We are witnessing the birth of a new world view. Out with the old; in with the new.

24

No Nuts in the Shell

Educational or vocational achievement is a prime indicator of life chances for non-white people in the United States. The central issue I raise in this chapter is did the Supreme Court decision Brown v. Board of Education improve the quality of life for African Americans nationwide? I have my doubts it did. I have doubts African Americans will ever rise above the nationwide education level in which we are presently situated. We should all be concerned that only 14% of students enrolled in colleges and universities are African American compared to being 38% of all persons incarcerated.[152] It's even worse California. The percentage of African Americans who are incarcerated in California state prisons is 29% compared to 2% black undergraduate enrollment in the UC system and 6% of the state population.[153] My doubts are further fanned by firsthand observations.

I observed over many decades that college students enrolled in my classes did not know the basic unit of a

---

[152] Status and Trends in the Education of Racial and Ethnic Groups 2018; The Bureau of Justice Statistics, June 14, 2016

[153] Public Policy Institute California, 2020

standard 12-inch ruler. The ethnic composition of my classes was diverse and so the inability of students to read a ruler was not disproportionately concentrated in one ethnic group or gender.[154] But I knew that even though my observations spanned decades I could not generalize that it reflected a failure of K-12 education for African American youth. So, I decided to do a survey and chi-square analysis of the survey data. My hypothesis was simple: the ability to read a standard 12-inche ruler is independent of gender. Based upon my classroom observations I thought that there was no difference of ability between girls and boys to read a 12-inch ruler.

Eight male and female students volunteered to go out to malls in Alameda County California with a standard 12-inch ruler. It was a good time of the year to do the survey because shopping malls during December are usually full of young people. With a predetermined point on the ruler, they were to randomly ask children between 15 and 18 a single question to help them measure the length of a line on a piece of paper. Female surveyors questioned female children and male surveyors questioned male students. They were to note yes for who could identify the point on the ruler or no, who could not identify the point on the ruler.

What the data revealed perfectly corresponded with my observations in classrooms over the years. It revealed that of the 160 students sampled 77% could not read a standard 12-inch ruler. The data also substantiated my hypothesis that the ability to read a 12-inch ruler is not

---

[154] I also observed that most did not know the basic unit of an analog clock which was posted on the classroom wall.

dependent on gender. The inability to read a standard 12-inch ruler means that children have not mastered the four arithmetic operations and their logical relations, their multiplication tables, division, fractions, and decimals. The simple fact is that there is a serious problem in the education pipeline. What has been popularized as the pipeline to prison is true. For some that pipeline leads to a lifetime of incarceration and reincarceration. For most others, it leads to an economic dead end. African American students are graduating or dropping out of school ill prepared for the kinds of livable wage jobs in the sciences and practical vocations. My findings parallel a study done in 2008-09. That study found that 82% "... never made it to a college-level math course;"[155]

Now, my thoughts turn to African American children. How badly are the education system and their families failing them? Our slave history demonstrates that family formation among slaves was prohibited by law. White supremacists understood that family has a positive effect on the formation of identity and serves as an indispensable network kinfolk for material support. Thus, they crushed it. At the same time, they understood that dominance is a function of educational, political, and economic control over time. If a lack of education could socially disable a percentage of white children, it would be disproportionately bad for African American children. But then I thought, wasn't that supposed to have been fixed 67 years ago by public school desegregation?

How problematic is it in the 21st century that most black

---

[155] The Numbers on California College degrees show blacks are 'being left behind', by Brenda Gazzar, May 28, 2015

children lack basic arithmetic competence nationwide? It is my view that it is very problematic and may accelerate our extinction in the United States by 2040. I understand that many African Americans don't want to think about that. But every day we stare at the effects of failed school desegregation policies as more and more young black men are socially disabled for life. As black marriage rates near zero and male and female high school dropout, incarceration, and jail rates disproportionately rise higher nationwide, all indications are that the 21st century is going to be extremely unfavorable to descendants of slaves.

If there are two statistics that tells us how important education is, it is that the average African American inmate in prisons and jails read at or below an 8th grade level and what Ph.Ds. African Americans are getting versus what Ph.Ds. they are not getting. Most blacks opt for a non-science Ph.D. or administrative education Ph.D. So, even at the HBCU campuses most Ph.Ds. teaching science and math are white or Asian persons. Even with HBCU schools for our youth, we couldn't operate without white people because we lack vital academic skill sets in the sciences. Benjamin Banneker and George Washington Carver are turning over in their graves.

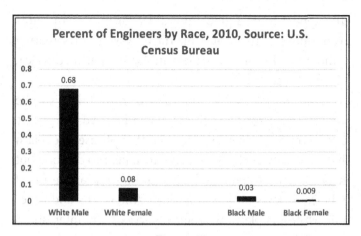

Figure 17

American law has not mitigated the education gap between non-white people and white people. It was never equipped to do so because it is based on English caselaw and statutes or in other words it is rooted in Aryan mythology. Its wheels are driven by the imprecise art of analogy. By that I mean American law is not a science, not necessarily logical, is amoral, and is bereft of any deep philosophical orientation or literary nature.

American Law is simply a caste technology used to preserve the status quo. If none of that were the case, U.S. history would be entirely different.

The legal system is one of many technologies white people have used to exercise their dominate caste power. So, whenever I think of the landmark Supreme Court decision Brown v. Board of Education, I try to figure out in what way did the court's decision serve the interests of white people in power. In the case of Brown v. Board of Education, the court's decision made the U.S. power elite appear to be a global moral leader in human rights even though at the same time the CIA were assassinating democratically elected leaders in Africa, Latin America, and the West Asia.

That is exactly the line of reasoning taken by the late law professor Derrick Bell when he used the phrase 'convergence of interests. He used that phrase to explain that white power elite know how to appear to do good but in fact intend to change long standing repressive racial policies or laws targeting African Americans and other non-white people only when it serves their interests to do so. White power elite change or repeal laws because it is in their best interests not because doing so is in the best interests of non-white people. And some policy and legal changes may even be reversed to offset old repressive policies and laws which over time become beneficial for African Americans.[156] Segregation is a case in point.

Segregation was obviously set up to discriminate against African Americans, to stunt them and keep them non-competitive and out of reach of opportunities. But ironically, segregation was having the opposite effect. It engendered more economic self-determination, self-sufficiency, and innovative excellence in places like Tulsa Oklahoma, Wilmington North Carolina, Rosewood Florida, etc., because we were left alone in our spaces and had to cooperate and be creative to collectively survive like all cultures do.

Black dollars didn't circulate in white communities

---

[156] Bell, Derrick Jr., Silent Covenants: Brown v. Board of Education and the Unfulfilled Hopes for Racial Reform, Oxford University Press, 2004

first; they cycled in and out of black families, businesses, and banks. They were exchanged for goods and services from person to person before leaving the black community. Adding to that growing wealth were some of the greatest athletes, musicians, and intellectuals in the world who lived within arm's reach in black segregated communities. Our segregated markets were ever so slowly growing and white supremacists looked at their socio/economic statistical models of black communities and saw cultural unity. They saw greater generation than corruption. They saw a live and competitive domestic economic and intellectual powerhouse. Those were bona fide unintended consequences of segregation. Their solution to what they perceived as a cultural threat to their dominance was desegregation. Courts went to work busting up a growing financial powerhouse in African American communities because now there was a quantitative divergence of interests.

First and foremost, I ask if what I've written is not true, then 'why hasn't the desegregation of public schools improved the general quality of life or life chances for more descendants of slaves in the United States? I think it's a relevant question to ask in what is a substantially changed world in the 21st century. But before I delve into the data which I think makes my question relevant, I will touch on a few of the educational challenges highlighted in the argument for desegregation in public schools made before the supreme court.

Descendants of freed slaves have been forced to live out their lives in social side shows throughout the history of the United States. Running parallel to white supremacist popular beliefs there were countless state laws instituted by whites which corralled descendants of freed slaves into urban race concentration camps. Eventually, legal federal segregation was reestablished by a Supreme Court Ruling 'Plessy v. Ferguson'.[157] That court's opinion turned on the issue 'whether segregated seating by race on trains violated a person's 14th amendment right of equal protection under the law'?[158] The court opined that if the seating arrangement were made 'substantially equal' in facilitation then segregation did not violate black peoples' civil rights to equal protection under the law. Thus, the 'separate but equal' rule became the law of the land.

That decision was yet another post-civil war setback for freed slaves.[159] But there was also another issue. It was the issue of whether deep psychological damage done to slaves, their children and freed slave grandchildren because of general racial segregation and their own internalization of white supremacists' beliefs. Irrefutable proof of deep psychological damage done to people of African descent would come from an experiment performed by Kenneth and Mamie Clark in the 1930s.[160] The findings of Kenneth

---

[157] The U.S. Constitution originally legalized segregation June 21, 1788.

[158] Attached to the 14th amendment is an enforcement clause intended to pre-empt states from circumventing the 5th amendment equal protection clause which was not applicable to the states.

[159] W.E.B. Dubois; Black Reconstruction, Black Reconstruction in America, 1935 by Harcourt, Brace and Co

[160] Kenneth B. Clark and Mamie P. Clark; Skin Color as a Factor in Racial Identification of Negro Preschool Children, Journal of Social Psychology, 1940, XI, 159-169

and Mamie Clark were a pivotal argument in Brown v. Board of Education.

Kenneth and Mamie Clark had a simple hypothesis. They claimed that "...racial identification [is a] function of ego development and self-awareness in Negro children."[161] Children's self-image and their feelings associated with it are a product of what frames their image in their environment. What frames it may be narratives, imagery, and behavioral responses to their spatial presence. The Clarks also stated that: "...racial identification is... related to the...genesis of racial attitudes in children... "[162]The Clarks concluded that "...color in a racist society was a very disturbing and traumatic component of an individual's sense of his own self-esteem and worth." I agree with their conclusion.

I summarize their findings this way. Early in childhood, African American children form a negative attitude about themselves. Children who attended segregated schools preferred white dolls and rejected black dolls saying black dolls were bad. When some of the 'black' children were asked to show the Clarks the doll that was most like them some of the children became so emotionally upset they ran from the room. But would Kenneth and Mamie Clark observe the opposite reaction by black children 67 years later? Tragically, no, they would not.

The late Dr. Derrick Bell who helped to fashion Critical Race Theory asked some important questions about the educational aftermath of Brown v. Board of Education in his book 'Silent Covenants'. Those questions are even

---

[161] Brackets mine
[162] Ibid

more pertinent today. He emphasized the fortuitous nature of our opportunities in the United States and the interest-convergence principle.

He defined it thus:

> "Rule 1. The interest of blacks in achieving racial equality will be accommodated only when that interest converges with the interests of whites in policy-making positions. This convergence is far more important for gaining relief than the degree of harm suffered by blacks, or the character of proof offered to prove that harm.

> "Rule 2. Even when interest-convergence results in an effective racial remedy, that remedy will be abrogated at the point that a policymakers fear the remedial policy is threatening the superior societal status of whites, particularly those in the middle and upper classes."[163]

So, if Bell was right, then Brown v. Board of Education was a fortuitous occurrence a collateral effect of complex intersecting global forces during the U.S. cold war with Cuba, China and the Soviet Union.[164] In other words,

---

[163] Derrick Bell; Silent Covenants: Brown v. Board of Education and the Unfulfilled Hopes for Racial Reform, Oxford University Press, 2004, pp. 69

[164] Mills C. Wright; The Sociological Imagination, Oxford University Press, 1956

there were converging interests between civil rights leaders and the U.S. Government at that time.[165] The white power elites wanted to appear to be a true democracy and justice oriented in comparison to communist and socialist nations. Given that, we should expect that the Supreme Court Decision in Brown v. Board of Education was only cosmetic and would not strike at the core of what causes our disenfranchisement.

At the core of what causes us to be disenfranchised is poverty and education. From the founding of the colonies and the United States we were imported as commodities to be used as a source of free energy or cheap labor. To buttress that purpose and after the civil war, we were legally excluded from every opportunity to thrive in the United States despite the 13th, 14th, and 15th amendments.[166] Congressional Enforcement Acts of 1870 through 1871 was needed to stop white supremacist KKK terrorism against us. My question to you is what political con has been played on us such that we are still fighting legal battles in 2021 which were won by three amendments to the Constitution and by Congressional Acts? The answer is because White Supremacy is alive and well in the United States.

Whatever national legal and institutional policy changes have occurred they were implemented to make us believe that we have progressed. But such changes always occurred within the context of a changeless caste

---

[165] Derrick Bell; Silent Covenants: Brown v. Board of Education and the Unfulfilled Hopes for Racial Reform, Oxford University Press, 2004, pp. 59

[166] The Maryland Doctrine of Exclusion, 1638

status for African Americans. Thus, there was progress but no substantive change for descendants of slavery. For us, there is no nut in the peanut shell.

Now, existential threats to African Americans transcend what legal options we may have. Those existential threats are increasing exponentially due to climate change. But at the micro level within the context of local life, a derivative and even more immediate existential threat faces descendants of slavery. That threat is the urban entropic effect. There are more socially disabled people in our neighborhoods than socially enabled people. Like the ratio of birth and death rates, that imbalance is a sure sign of impending ethnic extinction. The evidence towers over us at a tsunamic level.

Delipidated city infrastructure; the normalization of functional illiteracy by media; the loss of jobs which pay livable wages; increasing homelessness; mass incarceration and the correlative growth of a powerful anti-culture in black neighborhoods with its attendant degradation of more inner city children; food deserts and the correlative health problems such as diabetes and high blood pressure which stem from people's dependence on junk food; viral pandemics which have already caused a decline in the average lifespan of African Americans within 1 year; and white supremacists' mass co-optation of educated African Americans all portend a nightmarish disaster for descendants of slavery by the year 2040.

If at the end of the day politics boils down to self-interests and the necessity of immorality, then white supremacists power elite are absolutely and categorially concerned only with their interests not the suffering of and justice for descendants of slavery.[167] Thus climate change, all other things being equal, in these times of extreme global resource scarcity, I do not foresee descendants of slavery surviving in the United States beyond the year 2050. Neither do I foresee the survival of the United States of America through the 21st century. The path to that end will be tumultuous. It will pull the rug from under the feet of world powers flooring all players. As the U.S. declines in power, there will be a proportionate increase in an already inflated global power vacuum. That combined with climate change will make hell on earth for the scant hundred or so millions who cling to life.

---

[167] Hans J. Morgenthau; Politics Among Nations: The Struggle for Power and Peace, Pub. McGraw Hill, 1948

25

The Pandemic Doesn't Cause Violence

The national media is propagandizing the idea that the covid-19 pandemic is the cause of violent crimes across the United States. News clips show murder scenes in cities densely populated by African Americans. They suggest that there is an association between 'black on black' homicide and the Corona virus lockdown. That is a lie. But as you know, if the media repeats a lie enough times, then a percentage of people will start to believe it and quack out the same message to a larger percentage of other people. That is how Fox News and other media outlets operate to frame public opinion.[168] Lies like rumors can be contagious. Lies expressed through mass media in news and advertising trigger base emotions in crowds. Crowds then act out emotionally in the marketplaces of America, religiously, or politically.[169]

The truth is that the covid-19 pandemic is the cause

---

[168] Edward Bernays, Propaganda, Published by Ig Publishing,1928
[169] Le bon, Gustav, The Crowd: A Study of the Popular Mind, Pantianos Classics, 1896

of only two conditions: 1) infections and 2) deaths. For African Americans, it has resulted in over 87,391.[170] deaths or 18% of the total deaths in the United States. It has had some side effects too.

The pandemic has had an emotional effect on all of us. But while it has caused depression in thousands of people, another side effect of the pandemic is that it is causing an increase in compassion, cooperation, and empathy between strangers. Those are good side effects. They are the meaningful kinds of empathic feelings to human suffering we try to instill in every child.

The reasons for violence in our cities are a much more complex problem than viral infections are. Epidemiologists will figure out how the virus spreads, and its rate of spread. Statisticians will calculate the probability of death by race, age and gender. Biochemists will define the characteristics of the Corona virus, describe it RNA and how it invades our cells. And of course, a vaccine is now marketed for sale to mitigate the damage it can do to us. But, ironically, no one can devise a treatment for the historical and contemporary suffering of African Americans.

For example, how we socially organize in relation to one another; how densely populated we are in cities like Chicago and Harlem; how unequally income and wealth are distributed to us; how racist and repressive our society has always been to us; and how many men and women are incarcerated in prisons and jails for being black in America. Each play a part in causing violence in our

---

[170] Le bon, Gustav, The Crowd: A Study of the Popular Mind, Pantianos Classics, 1896

society. Black on black homicide is a function of all the above except the Corona virus lockdown. The Corona virus didn't cause those political and social problems; each of those problems predate the covid-19 pandemic by hundreds of years.

How many people in the United States are addicted to opioids or cocaine, or alcohol, and let's throw the crack epidemic in the pot, instigated and maintained by Uncle Sam? Search for a word like crazy to describe it and you'll fall short. The word crazy is not a strong enough word to describe the spiritual bankruptcy, the mental, and emotional dysfunction that black people suffer in cities across this nation. The virus didn't do any of that. The virus didn't cause descendants of slaves to be dysfunctional. White supremacy in all its manifestations causes descendants of slave to be dysfunctional. White supremacy has caused millions of African Americans to suffer personality and affect disorders defined clearly in the Diagnostic and Statistical Manual for social workers, psychologists, and psychiatrists. White supremacy has made millions of African Americans crazy.

For over a year, we were on house lockdown and suffered a stagnant national economy. But at the same time the prison industrial complex has had a million black men and women in jails and prisons on 24hr lockdowns for decades despite lack of medical care and Covid-19 infections. In truth, the economic sinkhole we are in was not caused by the covid-19 lockdown. The truth is there are no jobs which pay livable wages. There is a non-covid-19 reason for that. It is the new black code for incarceration. It is to lock up young black males. Lock up young black male high school dropouts. And Lock up young black males who are unemployed. If it sounds familiar that is because it is a redo of the old post-civil war black codes enacted by southern states[171]

Blue collar jobs have been taken away to nations all over the world but especially Asia and particularly to China. Over 5 million manufacturing blue-collar middle-class income level jobs were taken to a nation which now has a stronger economy than the United States. China is now the single world class power. U.S. corporations made China the new power even though China is governed by the Chinese Communist party. But China didn't kidnap U.S. corporations. U.S. corporations lusted for the Chinese consumer market potential and its cheap human resources. Meanwhile in post manufacturing cities like Oakland California, incarceration rates have increased in proportion to the loss of manufacturing jobs. As China grew, more black people were incarcerated. Therein lies the benchmark. The data is slapping us in the face.

Thirty-Three percent of African Americans and Latinos are federally defined as below the poverty line in East Oakland. It's like that across the nation. Throw into the pot high levels of child lead poisoning especially in the Fruitvale district and the crack epidemic, both instigated and maintained by Uncle Sam, and we are wanting for the words to describe the spiritual bankruptcy, along with mental and emotional dysfunction of descendants

---

[171] Daniel, Roderick Van Dr., Unjustifiably Oppressed: Black Codes of Mississippi (1865), Van Daniel Marketing, LLC, Aberdeen, Birmingham, DC, Memphis, Atlanta, Boston, 2018

of slaves and Latinos in the city of Oakland California. The virus didn't do any of that. Each of those pre-existing conditions to the virus will exist after the virus has faded into history.

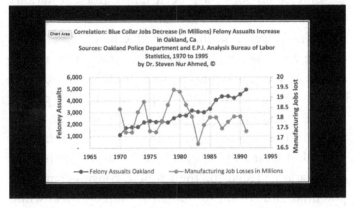

Figure 18

26

The Urban Entropic Effect

Considering what methods white supremacists have used in the past to kill innocent people, the major premise of my argument in this chapter is that the second law of thermodynamics (the transformation of anything from one form to another form results in non-usable waste) has been long understood by scientists and has been converted into practical social policies applicable to black men and women who have been digested or cycled through or who are cycling through our massive federal, state, county, and city prison systems. It's a very simple principle to understand. Let me explain by analogy.

The urban entropic effect is an artificially constructed set of social conditions to waste human lives for profit and to recycle them through a criminal justice system which operates on a private business model even if it is a public system. When an open pot of water is put onto a burner, the water heats and as the water evaporates it turns into steam. The energy (heat) that is lost in the form of steam is, when it flows into an open room, a measure of entropy because that amount of steam is unavailable to do work or be active in the liquid state in which it started. Families, neighborhoods, communities, cities, and whole nations are analogous to that process of entropy. Each group contains people. It is people who are damaged and lost when they are incarcerated. On a mass scale, that process destroys whole communities.

When people are taken out of their families and neighborhoods and then incarcerated, they are culturally transformed just as soldiers are emotionally and psychologically transformed when they kill people in wartime. A cultural transformation occurs whether they like it or not because their core values and world-view change.

When incarcerated people return to their communities, they are not socially, emotionally, and psychologically integrated. Incarceration makes them socially disabled for life. Thus, most of them are no longer socially useful and thus become part of an aggregate measure of disorder in a community. Many will lapse back into criminal lifestyles; others will become drug addicts or homeless. A very small percentage of them will against all odds wash the mud out of their subconscious and regain their emotional and psychological integrity like Malcolm X did. But overall, if cycled and recycled over time, families, neighborhoods, and communities will wobble out of control.

Sometimes the loss of human usefulness is unavoidable such as when there is a physical injury, illness, and/or old age. But, for African Americans the entropic process has been artificially sped up by race profiling, arrest, incarceration, release, and reincarceration cycle of which millions of African Americans are victims.[172] We are victims of an artificially constructed social experiment which was originally designed to stop the civil rights movement, and which has transformed whole sub-cultures into anti-cultures. If you are too young it is understandable that you cannot visualize that process. It is understandable why your frames of reference are what you hear on the news. That is part of the experiment. To bury you in short term memory news bits and pieces so that you cannot have the perspective needed to see the grand design. So that you miss the forest for the trees. But that is exactly what has happened to the African American community.

Never doubt the cleverness of elite white supremacists. Doing so could be a fatal mistake. It doesn't matter what your status is. You are in conditions designed by them; you are reacting to them directly or indirectly all the time. There are reasons for it being that way. They have had centuries of collective practical experience and scientific education passed down from one generation to the next. While we have struggled just to learn to read and write. So, their expertise in the sciences should not surprise anyone.

They know how to convert natural laws for practical purposes in social experiments using people as lab guinea

---

[172] The Oakland Police Department in California arrested 76,000 individuals over a 3-year period. Also see: Ferguson, Missouri. "...Ferguson...acts less like a municipality and more like a self-perpetuating business enterprise, extracting money from poor blacks that it uses as revenue to sustain the city's budget.", A City Where Policing, Discrimination and Raising Revenue Went Hand in Hand, by Campbell Robertson, New York Times, March 4, 2015

pigs.[173] They do it if doing so will be advantageous to their power or wealth interests. For example, the dropping of two atomic bombs on Japanese cities during World War II was not an act of war necessity; instead, it was a scientific experiment to determine the results of radiation exposure on civilian populations. They knew it would kill the aged, women and children. They wanted to kill them in that horrific way. They did the same to non-combatants using incendiary bombs on Tokyo, again, they knew it would kill the aged, women, and children. They wanted to kill them so that they could study their suffering.

Descendants of slaves have always been a threat of rebellion to white supremacists even in the slave labor concentration camps. They have always feared us; they fear the very thought of us. They fear the very image of us. But their fears were inflated even more in the 1960s because black demographics. The first wave of African American baby boomers was coming of age and impassioned and encouraged by new civil rights legislation. The end of redlining. The end of restrictive covenants. The end of segregated public schools. The end of segregated professional sports. Many strong leaders who were unafraid to voice our feelings to the world. Millions of young fearless African American youths posed a direct political and economic threat to the Aryan foundation of the United States. They were a threat to the white supremacist's status quo on many levels because it

---

[173] Medical Apartheid: The Dark History of Medical Experimentation on Black Americans from Colonial Times to the Present, by Harriet A. Washington, Anchor Books, New York, 2006

was African American baby boomers who gave thrust to the civil rights movement. It was they who made it happen. It was they who said white privilege must go.

Generally, African Americans are on an irreversible social track to ethnic identity extinction. There are many reasons for that. But nationwide, descendants of slaves are reeling from the urban entropic effect. The urban entropic effect is an artificially constructed set of social conditions used by white supremacists to stop the civil rights movement and to prevent it from ever happening again. They were formulated by the White House, Congress, F.B.I., and C.I.A. Those conditions were designed to counter social justice movements and the fear white supremacists had and still have of the civil rights movement and its leaders of the 1950s and 1960s.

Whole black communities are now designed to be prison feeders. For instance, in Oakland California over the course of 51 years or 2 ½ generations, so many African Americans have been cycled through jails or prisons that the composition of neighborhood blocks consists of larger and larger percentages of individuals who are socially disabled or unavailable to do work, can't start families or provided for children they have sired. That is one example of the urban entropic effect. From a macro perspective one can observe a correlation between that and increased disorder in some of the most historically fundamental institutions that are vital for stable and productive lives.

National and global economic changes have tightened the ball and chain around the ankles of 2 ½ generations of African Americans. The gradual loss of over five million manufacturing jobs called the exodus of capital out of the

United States occurred at the very time that Baby Boomers were coming of age in the 1970s was the starting line for a gauntlet of artificially constructed challenges meant to socially disable young black males.[174] Social planners could see in the demographic numbers that there would be no meaningful roles for most of them in the 21st century.

So, an institutional design was crafted to find a profitable place for socially marginalized people. For example, the inane removal practical courses such as weights and measures, woodshop, metal shop, mechanical drafting, and auto mechanics in public middle and high schools while manufacturing jobs were decreasing by the millions was a surreptitious way to construct the school to prison pipeline. Directly related to that 66% of the 33 California State prisons were built after 1970 at the very time the fourth wave of Baby Boomers were coming of age.[175] The role and place for millions of descendants of slaves was prepared.

Combine that with the large number of minority high school dropouts and the circumstances for millions of

---

[174] The Exodus of Capital: Between 2000 and 2010, US manufacturing experienced a nightmare. The number of manufacturing jobs in the United States, which had been relatively stable at 17 million since 1965, declined by one third in that decade, falling by 5.8 million to below 12 million in 2010 (returning to just 12.3 million in 2016).Wikipedia

[175] California Department of Rehabilitation and Correction, 2020

youths was made combustible.[176] For example, two thirds of California prison inmates are functionally illiterate. They read below a ninth-grade level. Thus, at least 114,180 thousand inmates in California State prisons are middle-school and/or high school dropouts.[177] That is irrefutable proof that the school to prison pipeline was designed and not the result of inherent character defects. That design had to be protected by law.

Legislation has always been used to exploit African Americans. The exploitative legal piler is Article 1, Section 2, Clause 3 of the U.S. Constitution. But periodically booster laws were needed as social circumstances changed. Richard Nixon's "war on drugs" according to John Ehrlichman was designed to criminalize black people just as the Constitution was designed to enslave African people.[178] Prison and jail populations increased from 300,000 to 2.3 million beginning in 1971.[179] Then in 1994 Congress passed the Violent Crime Control and Law Enforcement Act allowing President Bill Clinton to sign it into law. California had its repressive booster law

---

[176] High School dropouts are not counted as being part of a high school population. So, the numbers of children by high school age are incomplete. Consequently, the numbers of those completing high school and going to college as a present of the high school population is inflated. See for inaccurate data: U.S. Bureau of Labor Statistics: Percent of High School and College graduates, 2020, For Release, Tuesday, April 27, 2021

[177] California Department of Rehabilitation and Corrections

[178] "The Nixon campaign in 1968, and the Nixon White house after that, had two enemies: the antiwar left and black people.... Did we know we were lying about drugs? Of course,

[179] Equal Justice Initiative, eji.org

version, too. It is popularly called 'the three-strike law'. On March 7, 1994, Republican California Governor Pet Wilson signed into law AB 971. It legislated life in prison for a 3rd felony conviction.

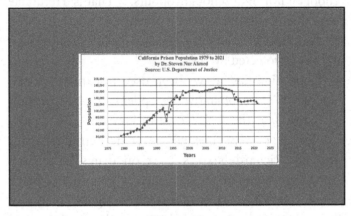

Figure 19

But the design to feed black youth into prison systems across the nation was even more intricately woven into the fabric of black lifestyles than one might see at first glance. In 1987, I watched Oliver North at a Congressional hearing admit that he flew a DC-6 plane full of 'humanitarian aid' back and forth from Nicaragua to the United States. His express purpose was to exchange drugs for money with which to buy weapons for the Contras in Nicaragua.[180]

---

[180] Nick Schou, Kill the Messenger: How the CIA's Crack-Cocaine Controversy Destroyed Journalist Gary Webb, Nation Books, New York 2006; see also, Gary Webb, Crack Plague's Roots are in Nicaraguan War, 1996, Libcom.org

The plane had been used by a well-known drug dealer to transport drugs back and forth from South America to the U.S. Oliver North said that the trafficking "is probably being used for drug runs into the U.S." The cocaine epidemic in black communities is directly related to President Ronald Reagan's arms and cocaine 'Contra-Scandal'.[181] The infusion of cocaine into black communities during the 1980s and 1990s accelerated the nightmare of crack addiction, destruction of families, incarceration, and death[182]

We have long passed the tipping point for reversing the multiplication of socially disabled people who are cycled through our prison and jail systems because of the disruption of the jobs market beginning in the late 1970s. As a result, the urban entropic effect has swollen to such an extent over the last forty years that the proportion of socially disabled people in most of our urban communities is now greater than the proportion of socially enabled people.

So influential is the prison yard anti-culture that children are now primarily socialized by it and multiply the problem even further as they adapt its language and lifestyles which are highly likely to socially disable them and thereby over time degrade communities even more.

---

[181] "John Kerry's 1988 Committee on Foreign Relations report on Contra drug links concluded that "senior U.S. policy makers were not immune to the idea that drug money was a perfect solution to the Contras' funding problems". Committee on Foreign Relations, 1988

[182] Jon Schwarz, Oliver North Worked With Cocaine Traffickers To Arm Terrorists. Now He'll be President of the NRA", May 12, 2018

When joined with the macabre national media spawned by it and glorifies it; and which is now the premiere form of popular mainstream entertainment in America. Any objective sociologist or anthropologist would conclude that African American culture and indeed the whole of America is spiraling downward out of control.

27

Generations to Come

There are several social phenomena which will affect generations of descendants of slaves to come. I consider them core life variables. They are 1) the fertility rate, 2) the marriage rate, and 3) the abortion rate. My thesis in this chapter is that if each of these rates remain negative or constant, they will cause the demise of the descendants of slavery population in the United States independent of any other factors.

The issue is controversial due primarily to the stance of the democratic party and white feminists' opinions dating back to the eugenicist Margaret Sanger. The practice of them is inconsistent with biological necessity despite interventionistic medical innovations which can safely alter the biological process. But so extreme are the threats facing us now, I am far beyond being concerned about opinions from any individual, other ethnic group or political party on the problems of black fertility, marriage, and abortion. In those matters, I am concerned solely with what is in the interests of black people not ideology.

Despite that, each variable is inherent in the demographic dynamic of descendants of slaves as they are in all populations. What I mean is that what will affect generations of descendants of slaves to come will be the results of our biological processes and personal choices today. We should not confuse our biology with our social conditions.

We should examine each variable independently and only afterward do a multivariate analysis to assess their combined effect on us. Historically, our social circumstances change from moment to moment, whereas our biology hasn't changed for millions of years. Thus, social circumstances may suddenly without warning change and become very life threatening. If a situation does become extremely life-threatening, then the probability for group survival may reduce entirely to this question: whether collective biological processes have been socially allowed to operate as naturally as possible from generation to generation?

In August 2020, the U.S. Census bureau reported that "...there were 46.8 million people in the U.S. who 'identified as Black as Black a 29% increase over almost two decades.[183]

However, the report goes on to say that "...there has been a more dramatic increase among the foreign-born population...10% of the Black population was foreign born." Ten percent of 46,800,000 is 4,680,000. Thus, the population of native-born Black people is reduced to about 42,120,000. Keep in mind that the offspring of foreign-born Black people who are of a different ethnicity would further reduce the number of Descendants of Slaves in the

---

[183] Key findings about Black America, By Christine Tamir, Pew Research Center, March 25, 2021

U.S. Even more important is the death rate of Black Baby Boomers at approximately 467 per day. That will draw down the 8,535,800 Black Baby Boomers who were born between 1946 and 1964 the total population through 2037.

The meaning of ASFR is *'age specific fertility rate'* the number of babies that would be born per one thousand to females between 15 and 45 yeas of age over the course of their childbearing years. For any human population to remain at a constant number, a fertility rate must be maintained at 2.2 babies born per female between the ages of 15 and 45. A number above 2.2 is a measure of population growth. Conversely, a measure which is below 2.2 is a measure of what is called technically 'decay'. Thus, no matter how large a population may be in the moment, a look beneath to its core generative power will reveal whether that group is in growth; whether it is stable; or whether it is in decline.

The method for calculating a fertility estimate is done by multiplying the sum of the percent (in decimals) for each age category by 5. The formula is:

$$TFR = 5 \, \Sigma \, ASFR$$

The following is my calculation for the ASFR for Descendants of Slaves 2019:

ASFR	Birth Rate
1. 15 to 19	0.016
2. 20 to 24	0.066
3. 25 to 29	0.093
4. 30 to 34	0.098

5. 35 to 39   0.053

6. 40 to 44   0.012

$$5(0.016+0.066+0.093+0.98+0.053+0.012) = 1.69$$

As of 2020, there has been a further 4% decline in the birth rate for descendants of slaves compared to 2019. The ASFR is currently 1.3 for black females 15 to 50.[184] The population of Descendants of Slaves is in irreversible decline.[185]

Percent Decrease Black Births 2019 to 2020

Year	Births	
2019	548,075	$\underline{528,448 - 548075} = -04\%$
2020	528,448	548,075

The western nations including Japan have all been measured at below a population replacement level of 2.2. Their populations are dying because of that. The age specific fertility rate of black people is trending exactly in sync with western nations. The western nations, including the United States, remedy is to import refugees from nations which they have been kept politically and economically dysfunctional since the colonial period. There is no remedy for black people in the United States.

The imitation of the slave master's lifestyles and various

---

[184] National Vital Statistics, Report No. 012, May 2021, by Brady E. Hamilton, Ph.D. et al. Division of Vital Statistic, National Center for Health Statistics

[185] Vital Statistics Surveillance Report, National Center for Health Statistics System Natality, 2020

ideologies by black people indicate that black people have no consciousness of what is in their own interests or if some do, they intentionally choose the opposite. But when put into perspective western ideologies and lifestyles are solely responsible for the anthropogenic ecological disasters, we are now experiencing all over the world according to the International Panel on Climate Change report released in 2021.[186] The irreversible ruination of life on Earth by the Western powers is reflected at the micro level in myriad ways but especially in the ruination of the African American population. Another element of population decline is the descendant of slave's marriage rate.

Heterosexual marriage among descendants of slaves has been in decline for over 70 years. That marriage trend is correlated with the population decline. That is a logical trend because for hundreds of thousands of years all men and women have had either life-time sentimental bonds sanctioned by their culture which at least intuitively legitimated enduring male female relations as opposed to lifestyles of sexual experimentation.

Enduring male female relations proved to have moral and existential value for small bands, tribes, and clans. Though marital forms varied from place to place, marriage and families gave rise to societies as well as provide order, continuity, and usefulness for the children born into networks of marital sentiment. There is no logical argument that can be made for a historical alternative to

---

[186] The Sixth Assessment Report, Climate Change 2021: Physical Science Basis, United Nations

heterosexual marriage with an equal long term existential value.

It is common knowledge that enslaved Africans were not allowed to marry and to form families. Slave owners knew that marriage engendered the existential value of strong family sentiment and the ordered rearing of children. So, they constructed social contexts in which emotional relations diametrically opposed to sentimental bonding could thrive. They instituted 'anti-sentiment' among slaves to be both a dominant and divisive emotion and to serve the informant interests of the slave owner.

Instead of heterosexual unity, they constructed a context which ignited polarity between men and women. Then, over time, they let gender polarity stew. Slowly it was institutionalized and normative behavior for boys and girls. Thus, they learned to despise each other's phenotype and gender from the preceding generation which reinforced and developed race and gender pejoratives. Consequently, subconscious self-hatred flourished among slaves and continues to this day. That subconscious hatred is only suspended temporarily to relieve the overpowering natural reproductive craving, but biological attraction alone does not bind us to one another emotionally.[187]

Today, we see the marriage data for descendants of slavery. It affirms a resurgence in self-hatred among black men women. The graph below demonstrates a steep decline in marriage among descendants of slaves from

---

[187] Orlando Patterson, The Sociology of Slavery: An Analysis of the Origin, Development and structure of Negro Slave Society in Jamaica, Fairleigh Dickinson University Press, London, 1967, pp.159, 162,164,165 footnote 5, 170

1950 at a 65% marriage rate to 2020 at a 23% marriage rate. That is a 42% decline in marriage among descendants of slaves over a period of 70 years or 2 ½ generations. If you look at the projection to 2050, you will see marriage at 0.04% among descendant of slaves.

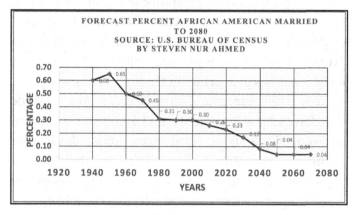

Figure 20

There are many factors which I could analyze to explain the current and projected marriage rate and why they differ so drastically from the marriage rate in 1950. But the relation which our marriage decline has with the age specific fertility rate of black women is correlated with the decline not only in marriage but in the subjective attitudes about marriage and family in the black community. We are on a slippery slope. These facts speak loudly about our social deprivation because we are not being educationally, economically, and morally sustained by stable social structures. Thus, once again, I must reiterate the point that our age specific fertility and marriage rates and their respective declines are in perfect sync with climate change projections made by the Intergovernmental Panel on Climate Change.[188] We are about to crash with the total global environment. If we do not reverse both trends, then we are headed for a nightmarish disaster because if my thesis that the core of any population is its generative power and whether it is in growth or decay or whether it is culturally ordered or disordered then these facts should be our Gabriel's Trumpet Call. Gabriel is sounding out a long tune because it also warns us of abortion in the black community.

The 1973 Supreme Court Decision Roe v Wade was driven by a Eugenicists' and Feminists' argument for women's rights or equal rights under the law for women.[189] The Roe v Wade decision implies that population dynamics can be artificially suspended without adverse social consequences to society. In essence it causes what the sociologist Emile Durkheim defined as anomie.[190] Anomie is a social state of normlessness and cognitive dissonance.[191] All cultural values are not socially constructed. Some cultural values grow out of our circadian rhythms like the need to sleep when we are tired and estrus when ovulation occurs. They are core values in the organic cycles of a population which are in fact teleological in nature.

There are naturally defined gender limits to what we

---

[188] The Sixth Assessment Report, Climate Change 2021: Physical Science Basis, United Nations, 2021

[189] Roe v Wade, 410 U.S. 113 (1973)

[190] Emile Durkheim, The Division of Labour in Society, 1893

[191] Leon Festinger, A Theory of Cognitive Dissonance, Stanford University Press, Stanford, California1 1957

can and cannot do. If laws frame pregnancy as a product of social construction, then a deep organic gender frame of reference is obscured. That in turn, given enough social choices by men and women, causes normlessness. Over time, it will result in the slow wilting of a population just as does a famine or drought. The Roe v Wade decision is antithetical to inescapable biological necessity. It has nothing to do with political rights and everything to do with human evolution.

I ask this the simple question: what was and is in the best interest of the African American Community? Maybe I can approach the answer to this by the negative. It never has been in the best interest of black women to follow white women and adapt their white supremacist ideals even when promoted for all women. Abortion has led us into the valley of a slow population and cultural death. The facts are clear. We don't marry and we choose not to have babies, and if we do conceive an embryo, we abort it. That is suicidal. There is a generational price to be paid. It is a price which we cannot afford.

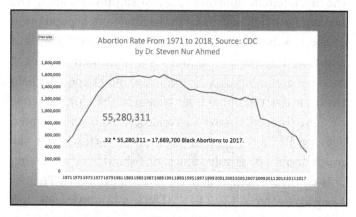

Figure 21

I stated that generative power is the core of every population and culture. I stated that it is sentiment or love which binds people and communities together for a lifetime and for generations to come. But when looking at figures like the ones above it is clear to me that there is an absence of mutual attraction in the black community.

Between 1979 and 2015, 17,600,000 (million) black fetuses were aborted. That is 32% percent of all abortions performed in the United States in that time span. Today, Black women constitute about 11.4% of all women in the U.S. That percentage is down from 12.3% in 2011-12. That constitutes a 7% decrease over 8 years. An almost 1% drop per year. It is due to abortion. The black abortion rate is 3 times the percentage of the black female population.

Look at it this way, if we add the number of the present population of descendants of slaves to the number of fetuses aborted, then our population would be about 57,500,000 (million) descendants of slaves in the United States today. So, it would be an understatement to say that the black female abortion rate is disproportionate to the percentage of black females in the total female population in the U.S. because of the long-term collateral effects of abortion. But maybe I should say it in as many ways as I can. We are in big trouble, and we should expect no help from the dysfunctional legal system in the United States.

The three vital rates I have described in this chapter, age specific fertility, marriage, and abortion rates say much about our family values, or I should say a growing anti-cultural orientation in the black community. There is a negative force at work in the black community which is greater than the core generative power of our population.

It is origin is situated in the individual and collective subconscious of millions of black Americans and acted out across the nation. For example, I just heard a report that there were 70 people shot and 10 killed in Chicago over one weekend.[192]

It is formed by white supremacists' culture in which we were born and raised. Insofar as the culture we are in is preferential to whiteness, it is simultaneously and automatically dismissive of non-white people except when non-white peoples have a convergence of interests with the power elite. Pretending to be accepted by white supremacists in the Republican or Democratic or Independent political parties twists those who do into morbid mannequin figures discussed by Franz Fanon in his book Black Skin White Mask but for which we pay the ultimate price of self-destruction and a lifetime of emptiness[193]

[192] 12 Killed, 70 People Shot Over Weekend in Chicago, Matt Masterson,| July 26, 2021

[193] Franz Fanon, Black Skin White Mask, Grove Press, New York, 1952

28

When Black Lives Don't Matter

Both public and private education has been a disaster for most African Americans nationwide. And the situation is so complex in urban schools that it would take a total crusade among all black parents to reverse a situation which right now is irreversible. It has been a disaster by design. Carter G. Woodson got it right when he stated that public and private schools' core purpose was/is to teach race propaganda to whites and non-whites to keep them either mentally caste dominate or subjugated.[194]

I remember a junior high school experience of mine at Havenscourt Junior High School in Oakland, California. I was placed in an 8th grade science class with about 40 other African American children. The class was decked out with lab tables and all the other paraphernalia needed for learning basic biology and chemistry.

As I reflect on my experiences there, it is clear to me that that science class lab and entire school was a left-over remnant of a past time. They were examples of what education was for white children compared to what it was

---

[194] Carter Godwin Woodson, The Miseducation of the Negro, Seven Treasures Publications, 1933

for us 'black' children. A well publicly maintained building infrastructure and qualified credentialed teachers were the norm. But that all changed upon black migrants' arrival to Oakland and our baby booming population.

The school was from a time before I was born when white children were taught there before 'white flight' out of Oakland.[195] It was a time when 100% of students at Havenscourt Junior High School were white. But the demographics had flipped. Though the building infrastructure remained well maintained because it was publicly owned our teachers were either less qualified or told not to teach to us except in shop courses.

Our science teacher was an African American male who did not have a degree in science. We had a science textbook, but not once in the year long course did, we study one chapter from the book nor do typical 8th grade experiments nor science excursions. Day after day we listened to him tell irrelevant stories about himself until one young sister became so frustrated that she shouted out "when are we going to do some science experiments!". I wish I could remember her name. The class was silent as Mr. Cleveland looked at her; he said nothing in response to her question instead he continued his usual irrelevant chatter. But even more telling, except for that young sister, none of us supported her rage. Something is wrong with the negro.

We were shuffled from that class to a math class. The teacher's name was Miss Carroll. She was an extremely

---

[195] Between 1950 and 1960, 100,000 whites fled Oakland to avoid 'black' people. They left well-maintained public-school building structures.

obese white woman. She exhibited absolutely no affect in a class of 13- and 14-year-old children. I realize now that many white adults do not perceive us as having a children hood. To them, we are just little 'blacks.' The extent of our math lessons consisted of coming into class and solving one long division problem everyday while Miss Carroll literally sat at her desk and cut paper figure cutouts with her scissors! I know because I sat in the front row in front of her desk watching her every day. She never lectured or explained any mathematical principles to us. Not one of us complained let alone parents. Something is wrong with the negro.

I finally got into the mind state of my sister in the science class. I was in an English class. It was riotous. The teacher again a white woman named Mrs. Smith. One day, I had had enough. I went up to her desk and told her I want to be transferred to a more challenging English course. She looked at me and I suppose decided to put the ball in more court. She selected a biography of about 200 pages. She said: Steven read this book and when you finish, I'll test you. If you pass the test, I'll get you into a higher course.

I took the book home and started reading. I read all night and into the morning until I finished it. The next afternoon during class, I went to her desk. I said to her that I'm ready for the exam. She looked surprised. I could see her eyelids open wide. She took the book and randomly selected pages asking me questions from each of them repeatedly. I answered her questions from each page to the letter. She looked at me with astonishment. I noticed as I was answering the exam problems that none of my classmates who I had known for years had the slightest idea of what was going on between me and Mrs. Smith. They were oblivious except for their class chatter with each other.

True to her word she wrote a letter to my counselor who happened to be a white male, Mr. Peterson, telling him what I had done and that he should put me in a college prep English class. He didn't say a word to me but instead wrote her a letter saying that there were no more available desks in those classes. At least that is what she told me. Of course, I felt dejected, and she knew it. I don't even remember what happened in that class for the rest of the year. It's all a blur. Not one of my teachers seemed to notice that I had just won the highest score 98.7% on the city American history examination and had been awarded by the school principal on stage in front of the whole student body. I wonder if it was personal. I'm being facetious. Deep down I was feeling the emotional aftershocks of the application of a white supremacist design.

It was the application of an educational tracking system based upon the revised Simon-Binet I.Q. test developed by a leading eugenicist Lewis Terman at Stanford University. It was a substructure within the public educational system designed to stunt our intellectual and emotional growth so that white children would have less academic competition from non-whites and become the scientists, sociologists, physicians, attorneys, and leaders of white supremacist society.[196] It has worked. Of all the scientist in the United States, 91% are White and Asian; 4.24% are Black. The

---

[196] Roberts v. The City of Boston, 1850

same percentages apply to virtually all the professions.[197] White supremacist elites wanted to dominate and own intellectual products as they dominated the land by owning all of it. No wonder most scientist are White people and work for at some level of government. The pay and benefits are good. There's high levels of prestige, status, and influential power along with white preferential treatment.

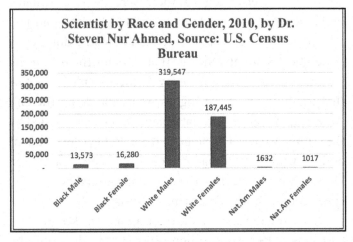

Figure 22

Most of us 'little blacks' back then were stone oblivious along with our parents to the institutional woodchipper machine we were being fed into. We were all damaged. We had no inkling of the scale of the psychological, physical, and emotional assault being made on us. I know from experience. I was physically assaulted by a white female

---

[197] Race/Ethnicity and Sex in U.S. Occupations, 1970-2010: Implications for Research, practice and policy. National Library of Medicine; National Institutes of Health, 2014

1rst grade teacher, I was denied food by a white female 4th grade teacher, I was punched in the stomach by a white male after school recreational director when I was 11 years old, and I was verbally ridiculed by an assortment of white male and female teachers. It continued in high school.

I attended Skyline Hight School in Oakland California. It had 60 black students out of a student body of 2,500 students in 1964 and had we not been bused to the campus there would have been maybe 10 black children on campus. I was so miserable there that had it not been for sports, I would have dropped out of Skyline High School my first year. White teachers blatantly ridiculed me in front of students in class and wrote in my academic record that I had no academic potential. I read it accidently.

I understand why most high schools in the United States post high dropout rates for African Americans males sometimes as high as fifty percent. It's a natural reaction to pain. For example, nationwide the black male dropout rate is 41%.[198] They drop out for the same reasons all of which are emotional. They get stressed out. That pain leaves lasting emotional scares and affects generations as trauma pours over into our babies' lives. What comes after us are cultural values, attitudes, and habits about education which are self-perpetuating and thus difficult if not impossible to change on a mass scale. For each of us, it gets deep down and personal. It is a uniform pattern pointed to by all anthropologists that people stay in groups wherein they are sustained emotionally and in which they are given and find value in themselves. Gangs in prisons and on the streets of America do that.

---

[198] https://www.sreb.org

Why can't K-thru-12 schools? You know the answer that question. Colleges and Universities fare no better unless a black student athlete is raking in millions of dollars for the school.

Though the number of African Americans enrolling into colleges and Universities has increased over several decades their completion of college rates have decreased. If one does not finish college, it's as though one never entered college because it cannot be put on one's resume. The pattern is repeated at every educational level. At Universities, 44.6% of African Americans drop out and do not earn their bachelor's degree.[199] Usually, African Americans feel isolated and implicitly unwelcomed by white students, faculty, and administrators on University campuses.

I remember an incident which occurred while I was attending California Poly-Technic State University, San Luis Obispo. It is a state University which recently recorded only 2 or 3 of its student body of more than 20,000 students as being black and they may have been immigrants. On Friday nights there was usually a motion picture shown in the student auditorium. It was convenient to attend if one was staying in the dormitories. So, one Friday evening I went. I sat down and watched the first 20 minutes of a movie which turned out to be Birth of a Nation by D.W. Griffith. It is one of the most racist movies of the early 20th century. Full of race stereotypes which last to this day.

I watched the white student reactions to the movie as it played. They were in awe of the scenes and clapped

---

[199] Completing College by Race and Ethnicity, 2017, Nscrecearchcenter.org

for the KKK episodes which glorified them. I got up and left. I was the only black student in the auditorium which was completely full of over 1000 students in attendance. It was 1976. The civil rights movement, Congressional Civil Rights Acts, and assassinations of Dr. King, Medgar Evers, and Malcolm X had not made a dent in the white conscious identification with white supremacy. White, Asian, and Indian students dominate every University and College campus in the United States. They are subconsciously and some consciously white supremacists. They assume black inferiority.

A few hundred black students on campuses like that can feel the negative 'vibes' and hear the propaganda spewed out by teachers especially in the liberal arts classes. At U.C. Berkeley in an Arabic class I took, a graduate student instructor who was an Iraqi Jewish female immigrant told the class a demeaning joke about black people and Cadillacs. There were two blacks including me in the class of about 70 students. Her insensitivity to our presence was cold and callous. Never mind that white people have always and to this day owned most Cadillacs in the United States.

In 1991, I organized an alcohol and drug abuse seminar for Castlemont high school students. The principal and teachers were extremely cooperative in helping those of us doing outreach for the West Oakland Health Council. The principal informed me that she mailed over 1000 announcements and invitations to every parent of every child at the school. We wanted it to be a family learning experience. We set up the seminar in the school cafeteria and exhibited booths from dozens of health providers in the city of Oakland. Afterward we then convened an assembly wherein numerous speakers spoke to the students about substance abuse and the lifelong health and social disabilities it causes millions of people and their families to suffer. Local news agencies were there because everyone knew that Castlemont was surrounded by liquor stores from which children were accessing alcohol and coming to school inebriated. I'm telling this story so that I can drive home a point about education. I don't think Carter G. Woodson wrote about this kind of problem. Maybe he could not envision the crack cocaine holocaust which was to sweep through the cities of America destroying millions of black lives.

After the close of the seminar, the Principal approached me and informed me that out of all the parental invitations she had mailed out only 1 parent attended the seminar. One in a thousand. We had worked so hard to make it a community learning experience. But parents were not interested. That is the lead to my concluding remarks in this chapter. If parents don't care about their children's plight and their educational institutions, then no school will ever succeed in facilitating those students who need help most. Let me share a small study I conducted in 2019.

I reasoned that if during slavery black codes were passed to prevent our ancestors from reading and writing because white people feared our intelligence and would whip slaves if they did learn, then today its mathematics and science which white supremacists don't want our children to learn. I am convinced of that because I had long known that Benjamin Banneker who was black and a self-taught mathematician contradicted everything negative said about black people's intelligence in 18th century America. Such was Banneker's genius that he wrote the first Farmer's Almanac used by agriculturalists up until the 20th century.[200]

In fact, Banneker wrote many books and papers on mathematics besides his Farmer's Almanac. Now, here is my point. On the day of his funeral, as his body was being carried to his grave, a group of white supremacists burned his house and every book in it to the ground. We lost his legacy in those flames. They didn't want us to inherit his legacy just as they didn't want us to inherit the legacy of ancient Kemet. Their grand purpose was for us to believe their eugenical propaganda about our having low intelligence. If 91% of all scientists in the United States are White and Asian, then that is what they want to monopolize and control. They don't want us to know science and mathematics and with it to produce knowledge because knowledge is another facet of power.

Let me share a small study I conducted in 2019. I was determined to find out if our children between the ages of 13 and 18 could identify a point on a 12-inch ruler. Some students at an east bay community college I taught at volunteered to do a survey. The hypothesis of the study was that there is a difference between boys' and girls' ability to read a 12-inch ruler. It's an important test because the ability to read a 12-inch ruler is evidence that basic arithmetic skills have been mastered and that a student is more likely to have the confidence to do algebra which is the gateway to higher mathematics. Mathematics

---

[200] Lisa M. Bolt, Benjamin Banneker: Self-Educated Scientist (STEM Scientists and Inventors), Capstone Press, 2018

is in turn the gateway to all the sciences and professions and thus a higher quality of life. It all begins at home and in about the 3rd grade. There are no more 'Black Codes' but there is a hidden curriculum in all public schools.

The data I collected compelled me to accept my hypothesis that boy's and girl's ability to read a standard 12-inch ruler are independent of gender. The data collected by my students consisted of 160 randomly selected teenage girls and boys. After I did a Chi-Square analysis, we found that 77% of the children irrespective of gender could not read a 12-inch ruler. Could this be associated with the very low percentage of African Americans in professions like engineering and architecture?

Though my survey consisted of a very small sample size, it at least raised for me some serious questions. One of which is whether that is evidence of the hidden curriculum? If this pattern holds true across the nation, then it's as though by design black children generally are not taught arithmetic. How is it that African American students enter and exit K-12 public schools and then graduate or drop out without knowing how to read a 12-in ruler? Do you want a larger sample size to prove my thesis? Test all black men and women entering state prisons nationwide. Give them a ruler and ask them to identify a point on it. It's a simple binomial question. Either they can or they can't.

If current data is accurate, incarcerated black men and women read at or below the 8th grade level. That means there is a higher than 50% probability that they cannot read a 12-inch ruler. Given that and the nearly zero turn out of parents at the Castlemont High School alcohol and drug abuse seminar I organized in 1991, I then knew that the problem is cultural and rooted in the homes of hundreds of thousands of our children nationwide. Far too many parents are not helping the cause to uplift the children of descendants of slavery. Why do I say African Americans are on the event horizon? Because no black organization whether religious or secular has been able to penetrate that core of the black community to terraform its culture so that it can grow.

Bibliography

Bary, John M. *The Great Influenza: The Story of the Deadliest Pandemic in History.* Penguin Booiks, 2005.

Bernasconi, Robert. *"Kant as An Unfamiliar Source of Racism," Philosophers on Race: Critical Essays, Julie K. Ward & Tommy L. Lott, editors.* Malden: Blackwell, 2002.

Blow, Charles M. *The Devil You KNow: A Black Power Manifesto.* HarperCollins, 2021.

Blumenbach, Johann. *On the Natural Origin of Human Variety.* Germany, 1775.

Bolt, Lisa M. *Benjamin Banneker: Self-Educated (STEM Scientists and Inventors).* Capstone Press, 2018.

Bon, Gustave Le. *The Crowd: A Study of the Popular Mind.* Pantianos Classics, 1896.

Boniacich, Edna. "A Theory of Ethnic Antagonism: The Spit Labor market." *American Sociological Review* (1972): 37.

Butler, Smedley D. *War is a Racket.* Los Angeles: Feral House, 1935.

Calhoun, John B. "Population Density and Social Pathology." *Scientific American, Inc.* (1962).

—. "Population Density and Social Pathology." *Scientific American* (1962): 80-88.

Ceballos, Gerardo. "Accelarated Modern Human-Induced Species Losses: Entering the Sixth Mass Extiction." *Science Advances* (2015).

—. "Accelerated Modern Human-Induced Species Losses: Entering the Sixth Mass extinction." *Science Advance* (2015).

Change, InterGovernmental Panel on Climage. "The Special Report on Climate Change and Land." Climate Change. 2019.

Clark, Kenneth B. Clark and Mamie P. "Racial Identification and Preferences in Negro Children, Socialization of the Child." *Journal of Social Psychology* (1940): 10(4):591-599.

Coline Raymond, Tom Mathews, and Radley M. Horton. "The Emergence of Heat and Humidity too Severe for Human Tolerance." *Science Advance* (May 08, 2020): Vol. 6, no. 19.

Dan Moore, Sr., & Michele Mitchell. *Black Codes In Georgia.* Atlanta: APEX, 2006.

Daniel, Roderick Van. *Unjustifiably Oppressed: Black COdes of Mississippi (1865).* D.C.: Van Daniel Marketing, LLC, 2018.

Dollard, John. *Frustration and Aggression*. Greenwood Press, 1939.

Donella H. Meadows, Dennis L. Meadows, et al,. *Limits to Growth, A Report of the Club of Rome's on the Predicament of MankindC*. Club of Rome, 1974.

Dubois, W.E.B. *Black Reconstruction in America, 1860 to 1880*. Free Press, 1935.

Durkheim, Emile. *The Division of Labor in Society*. 1893.

Fanon, Franz. *Black Skin, White Mask, *. New York: Grove Press, 1952.

—. *Black Slkin White Mask*. New York: Grove Press, 1952.

Festinger, Leon. *A Theory of Cognitive Dissonance*. Stanford: Stanford Univeristy Press, 1957.

Foucault, Michel. *Discipline and Punish: the Birth of Prison*. London: Penguin, 1935.

Frazier, E. Franklin. *Black Bourgeoise*. Free Press, 1962.

Garrett, T.J. "How Persistent is Civilization Geowth?" (2011): arXiv:1101.5635vl.

Gobineau, Count Joseph De. *Essay on the Inequality of Human Races*. 1853.

Goffman, Irving. *Asylum: Essays on the Social Situation of Mental Patients and other Inmates.* Anchor Books, 1961.

—. *Ayslums: Essays on the social Situation of Mental Patients on Other Inmates.* Anchor Books, 1961.

Gottschalk, Marie. *The Prison and the Gallows: the Politics of Mass Incarceration in America.* Cambridge Univeristy Press, 2006.

Hans J. Morgenthau, Reivised by Enneth W. Thompson and W. David Clinton. *Politics Among Naions: The Struggle for Power and Peace.* McGraw Hill Higher Education, Seventh Edition, 2006.

Hegael, George Wilhelm Friedrich. *The Philosphy of Right.* 1520.

Isenberg, Nancy. *White Trash: The 400-Year Untold History of Class in America.* Penguin Books, 2016.

John Dollard, Neal Miller, Leonard Doob, Orval Mowrer, Robert Sears. *Frustration and Aggression.* Yale University Press, 1939.

Jr., Derrick Bell. *Silent Covenants: Brown v. Board of Eduction and the Unfulfilled Hopes for Racial Reform.* Oxford University Press, 2004.

Kump, Micheal E. Mann and Lee R. *Dire Pedictions: Understanding Climate Change.* Penguin, 2008, 2015.

Lasswell, H. *Politicis: Who Gets What, When How?* New York: McGraw-Hill, 1936.

Luckmand, Peter Berger and Thomas. *The Social Construction of Reality.* Anchor Books, 1967.

Malthus, Thomas. *An Essay on the Principle of Population.* 1798.

Masson, Andre. *Journal of Economic Perspectives* (1989): Vol. 3, No. 3, pp. 141-152.

Mendel, Johann Gregor. *Experiments in Plant Hybridization.* 1866.

Merton, Robert K. "Discrimination and the American Creed." *In R.M.MacIver (Ed.), Discrimination and National Welfare* (1949): pp. 99-126.

Mills, C.Wright. *The Sociological Imagination.* Oxford University Press, 1956.

Myrdal, Gunner. *The American Dilemma.* New York: Harpper and Row, 1944.

Patterson, Orlando. *The Sociology of Slavery: An Analysis of the origin, Development and Structure of Negro Slave Society in Jamaica.* London: Fairleigh Dickinson Univeristy Press, 1967.

Plato. *The Republic.* n.d.

Poliakov, Leon. *The Aryan Myth*. New York: Barnes & Noble's Books, 1971.

Ravenstein, E.G. *Law of Migration*. Royal Statistical Society, 1885.

Rifkin, Jeremy. *The End of Work: The Decline of the global Labor FOrce and the Dawn of the Post-Market Era*. New York: Putman's, 1995.

Self, Robert O. *American Babylon*. Prinsceton University Press, 2003.

Snowden, Frank M. *Epidemics and Society: From the Black Death to the Present*. London: Yale University Press, 2019.

Totten, Samuel. *Century of genocide, Critical Essays and Eyewitness Accounts*. New York: Routledge Falmer, 2009.

Washington, Harriet A. *Medical Apartheid: The Dark History of Medical Experimentation on Black Americans from Colonial Times to the Present*. New York: Anchor, 2006.

Weber, Max. *Economy and society: An OUtline of Interpretive Sociology*. University of California Press, 1922.

Weiss, Harvey. *Megadrought and Collapse: From Early Agriculture to Angkor*. New York: Oxford University Press, ed. 2017.

Wilhelm, Sidney W. *Who Needs the Negro*. Garden City: Doubleday and Company, 1971.

Woodsson, Carter Goodwin. *The Mis-Education of the Negro*. Washingington D.C.: Seven Treasures Publications, 2010.

Printed in the United States
by Baker & Taylor Publisher Services